KETTLE'S YARD HOUSE GUIDEBOOK

KETTLE'S YARD

HOUSE GUIDEBOOK

Written and edited by Inga Fraser
Photographs by Gilbert McCarragher

Kettle's Yard, University of Cambridge

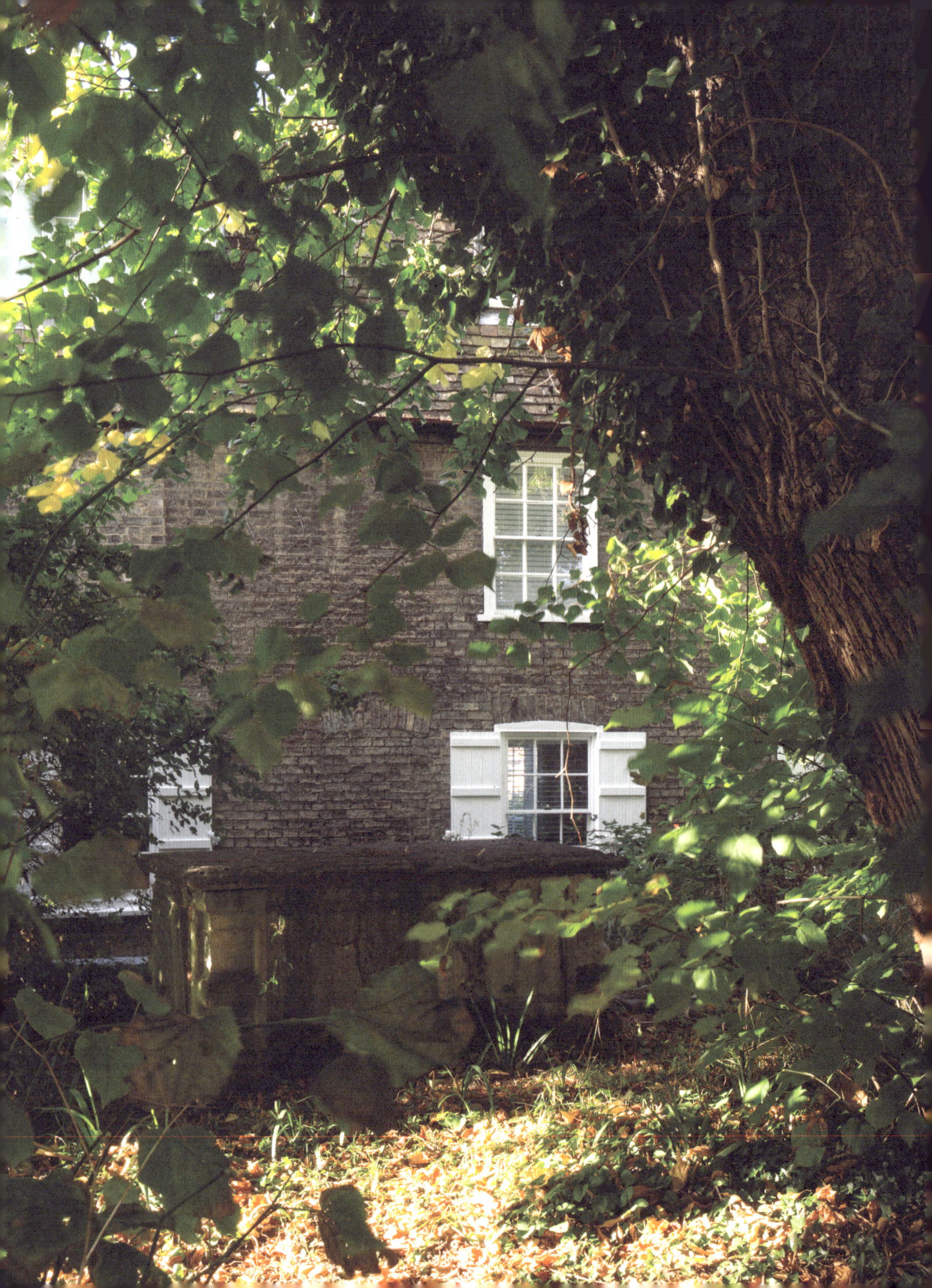

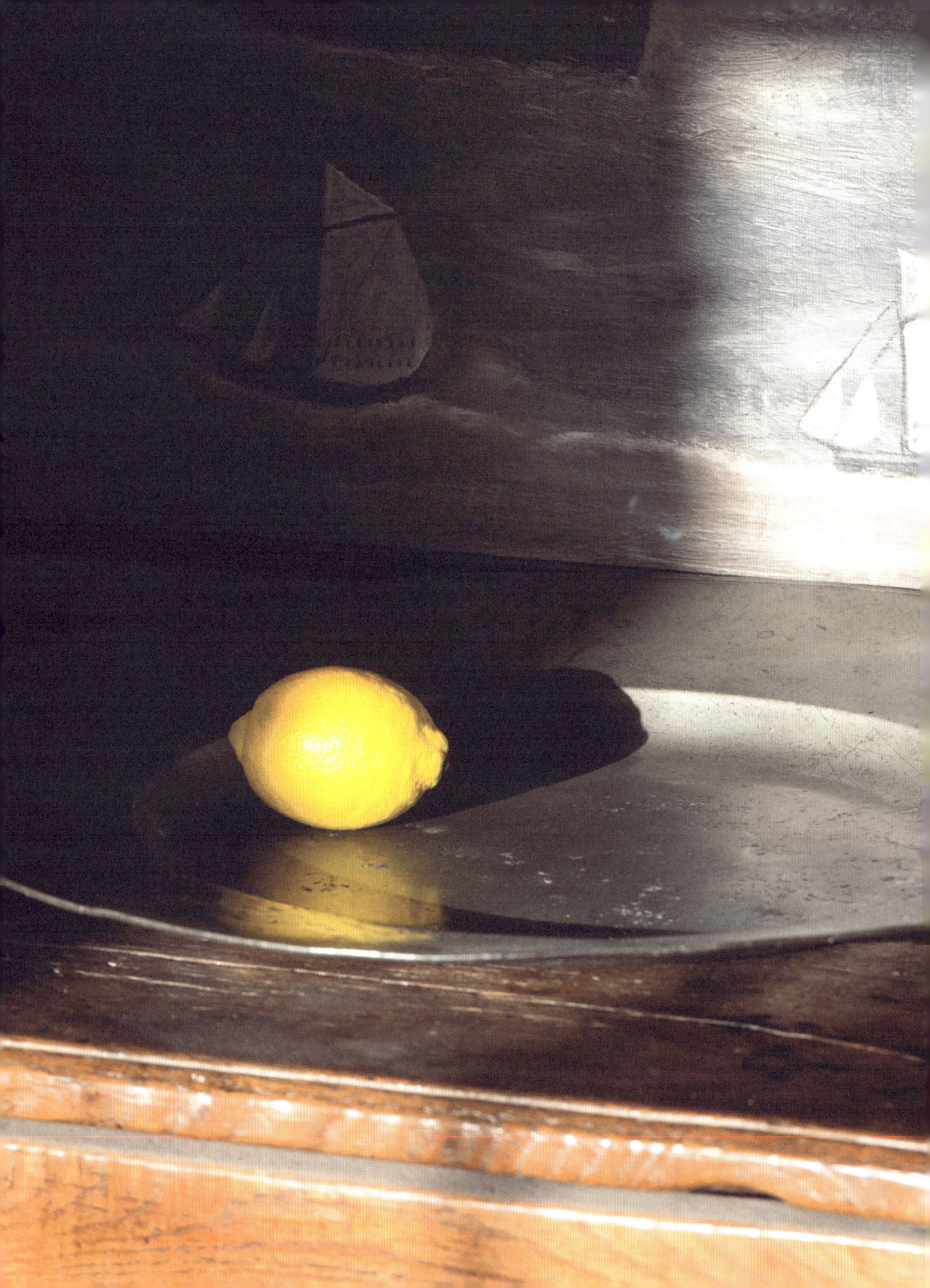

FOREWORD

Kettle's Yard is a remarkable place, created by a remarkable man. In a quiet corner of Cambridge, overlooking St Peter's Church, is a beautiful house filled with beautiful objects. It was once the home of H.S. (Jim) Ede and his wife, Helen, and still houses their collection of twentieth-century art alongside found and natural objects, ceramics, glass, textiles and furniture. Over 100 artists are represented in the collection. It includes works by Constantin Brâncuși, Naum Gabo, Henri Gaudier-Brzeska, Barbara Hepworth, David Jones, Joan Miró, Henry Moore, Ben Nicholson, Winifred Nicholson, Alfred Wallis and Christopher Wood. The contents of the house and their display reflect Jim Ede's life and travels, his friendships with leading artists of his time, his eye for found objects and affinity with nature.

The Edes lived at Kettle's Yard for over fifteen years, welcoming visitors into their home every afternoon. They hosted concerts in their tiny upstairs living room, and later in the 1970 extension designed by David Owers and Leslie Martin, one of the architects responsible for the Royal Festival Hall on London's South Bank. The extension included the first of a sequence of small galleries for temporary exhibitions. In 2018, new galleries and an education wing, designed by Jamie Fobert Architects, opened to critical acclaim. Today, Kettle's Yard hosts an ambitious year-round programme of exhibitions, events and activities.

Jim and Helen Ede gave the house and its contents to the University of Cambridge in 1966. It remains, by and large, how they left it. There are artworks in every corner, but no labels. A pewter plate still holds a single lemon, placed to balance a spot of yellow in the Miró painting hanging on the adjacent wall. Every day except Mondays, visitors are welcomed into the house, much as the Edes would have welcomed them. Jim Ede encouraged visitors to sit and spend time here, to pay as much attention to a worn broom head or the play of afternoon light as the drawings, paintings and sculptures in every room.

Today, the Kettle's Yard house is widely recognised as a masterclass in curating, a flawless arrangement of art and objects. In seeking to fuse art with life, Kettle's Yard has that rare power of changing how we see the world and our place within it.

— Andrew Nairne, Director, 2026

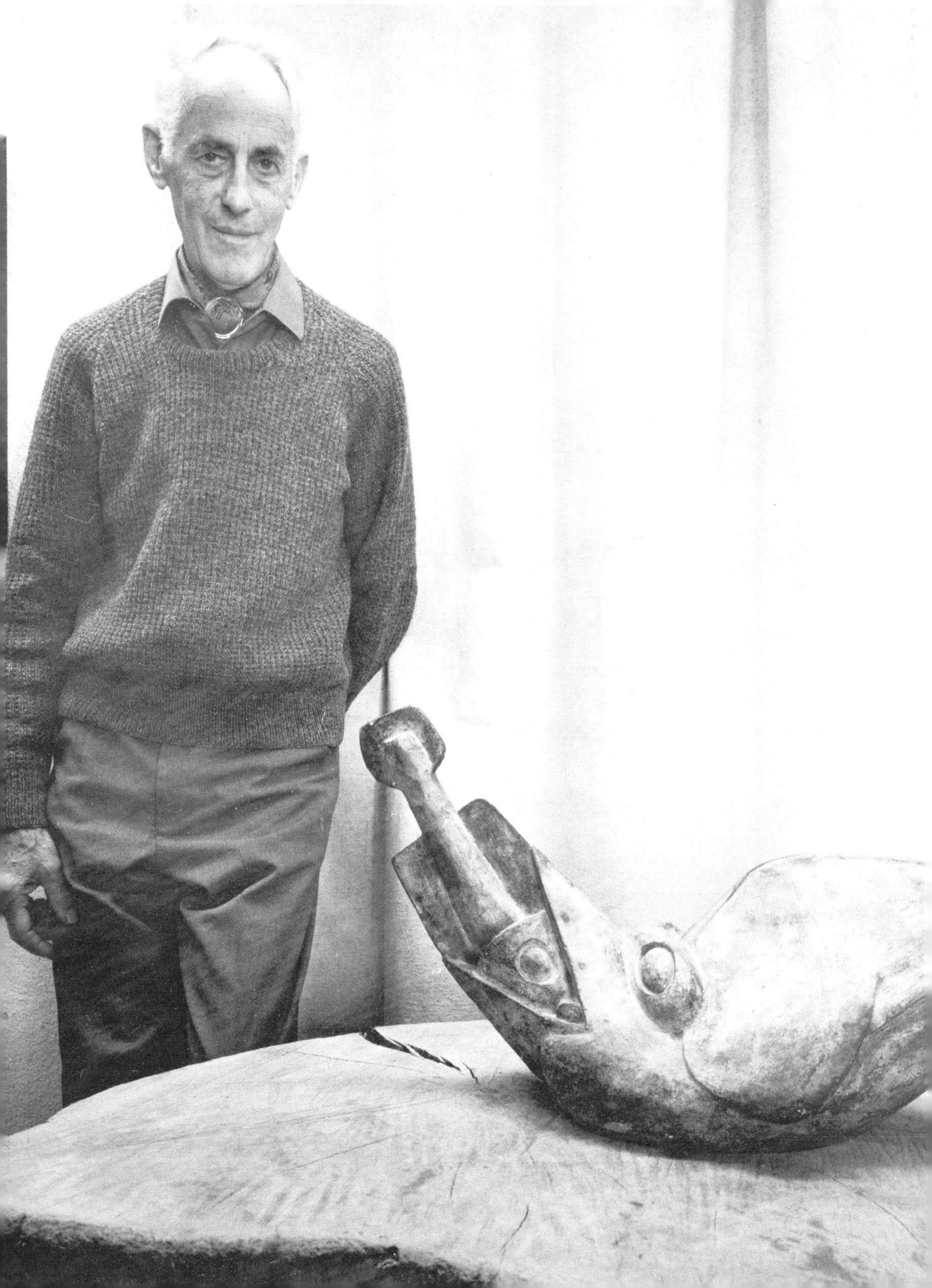

INTRODUCTION

JIM EDE, 1968

I have been asked to write a personal note on how Kettle's Yard was formed. I suppose it began by my meeting with Ben and Winifred Nicholson in 1924 or thereabouts, while I was an Assistant at the Tate Gallery. It started of course before that; I was fifteen at the Leys School in Cambridge and fell in love with early Italian painting and broke bounds to search the Free Library and Fitzwilliam Museum, and before that at thirteen when I first visited the Louvre, saw nothing, but fell for Puvis de Chavannes near the little church of St Etienne du Mont.

So it wasn't until I was nearly thirty that the Nicholsons opened a door into the world of contemporary art and I rushed headlong into the arms of Picasso, Brâncuși and Braque; not losing, however, my rapture over Giotto, Angelico, Monaco and Piero della Francesca. Ben Nicholson shared this rapture and I saw in his work a simple continuity from them into the everyday world of the twenties and thirties. There was no longer a break. Oddly enough I turned out to be one of Ben Nicholson's very few admirers at that time, and after he had tried to sell a painting for a year or so he would tell me that I could have it for the price of the canvas and frame, usually one to three pounds. I could not always manage it, for my salary was under £250 a year; not much to maintain a family in London. Many he would give me, and now that Kettle's Yard has been catalogued I find it has forty-four works by him, and many others have been given away. Winifred Nicholson taught me much about the fusing of art and daily living, and Ben Nicholson that traffic in Piccadilly had the rhythm of a ballet, and a game of tennis the perfection of an old master. Life with them at once seemed lively, satisfying and special.

Then came Kit [Christopher] Wood and David Jones. From Kit I learnt a clarity of perspective in regard to contemporary painters; a direct enjoyment, spontaneous and easy, which became a touchstone in the world of what has often been called naive painting; and so came Douanier [Henri] Rousseau and with him no doubt many works now held by Kettle's Yard. David Jones was different, he brought shape to the ephemeral in me, his profound vision of essential truth supported me. He had a tolerance not usual in artists and this enlarged my vision.

Jim Ede at Kettle's Yard with Henri Gaudier-Brzeska's *Bird Swallowing a Fish* photographed by Derry Moore, 1971

I think it was in 1926 I first began to get paintings by Alfred Wallis. They would come by post, perhaps sixty at a time, and the price fixed at one, two or three shillings according to size. I once got as many as twenty but usually could not afford so many. I suppose that Kettle's Yard now has a hundred.

In that same year I first heard of Henri Gaudier-Brzeska. A great quantity of his work was dumped in my office at the Tate: it happened to be the Board Room and the only place with a large table. It was ten years after Gaudier's death and all this work had been sent to many art experts for their opinion, and London dealers had been asked to buy. It had become the property of the Treasury and the enlightened Solicitor General thought that the Nation should acquire it, but no, not even as a gift. In the end I got a friend to buy three works for the Tate and three for the Contemporary Art Society, and the rest, for a song, I bought. Since then it has seemed my task to get Gaudier established in the rightful position he would have achieved had he lived into this present time. The principal collections of his work today are the Tate Gallery, the Musée National d'Art Moderne in Paris and Kettle's Yard, and he will surely, in time, be recognised as one of France's greatest sculptors and probably the most vital of his epoch.

Thus we come to 1936 when, save for the period of the Second World War, I left England for twenty years, living in Morocco and France and lecturing on art all over the United States. This brought me to Richard Pousette-Dart, a passionate follower of Gaudier-Brzeska and to William Congdon whose paintings of Venice at last exorcised Sargent and brought me back to Bellini. In England there was William Scott, Roger Hilton and recently Bryan Pearce. It was while we were still abroad in 1954 that I found myself first dreaming of the idea of somehow creating a living place where works of art could be enjoyed, inherent to the domestic setting, where young people could be at home unhampered by the greater austerity of the museum or public art gallery and where an informality might infuse an underlying formality. I wanted, in a modest way, to use the inspiration I had had from beautiful interiors, houses of leisured elegance, and to combine it with the joy I had felt in individual works seen in museums and with the all embracing delight I had experienced in nature, in stones, in flowers, in people.

These thoughts were greatly encouraged by American activity, by the Phillips Memorial Gallery and by Dumbarton Oaks;

homes made public and vital by continued enterprise. But how could this be managed without money? I tried for a 'Stately Home' which might become a source of interest to some neighbouring university and in the end was recommended by the President of the Cambridge Preservation Society, the use of four tiny condemned dwellings. So Kettle's Yard began. This was in 1957.

By keeping 'open house' every afternoon of term something was gradually developed which in 1966 was accepted by the University whose intention it was to continue this activity in its present form. On 5 May 1970 a large extension, designed by Sir Leslie Martin and his associates, was opened by His Royal Highness The Prince of Wales, and an inaugural concert was given by Jacqueline du Pré and Daniel Barenboim.

Kettle's Yard is in no way meant to be an art gallery or museum, nor is it simply a collection of works of art reflecting my taste or the taste of a given period. It is, rather, a continuing way of life from these last fifty years, in which stray objects, stones, glass, pictures, sculpture, in light and in space, have been used to make manifest the underlying stability which more and more we need to recognise if we are not to be swamped by all that is so rapidly opening up before us.

There has always been this need, and I think there always will be; it is a condition of human life, and in Kettle's Yard, which should I think, grow and change only very slowly, I hope that future generations will still find a home and a welcome, a refuge of peace and order, of the visual arts and of music.

On my side, I have felt strongly my need to give to others these things which have so much been given to me; and to give in such a way that by their placing and by a pervading atmosphere one thing will enhance another, making perhaps a coherent whole, in which a continuity of enjoyment, in the constantly changing public of a university, can thrive. Perhaps from it other ventures of this sort may spring. There should be a Kettle's Yard in every university.

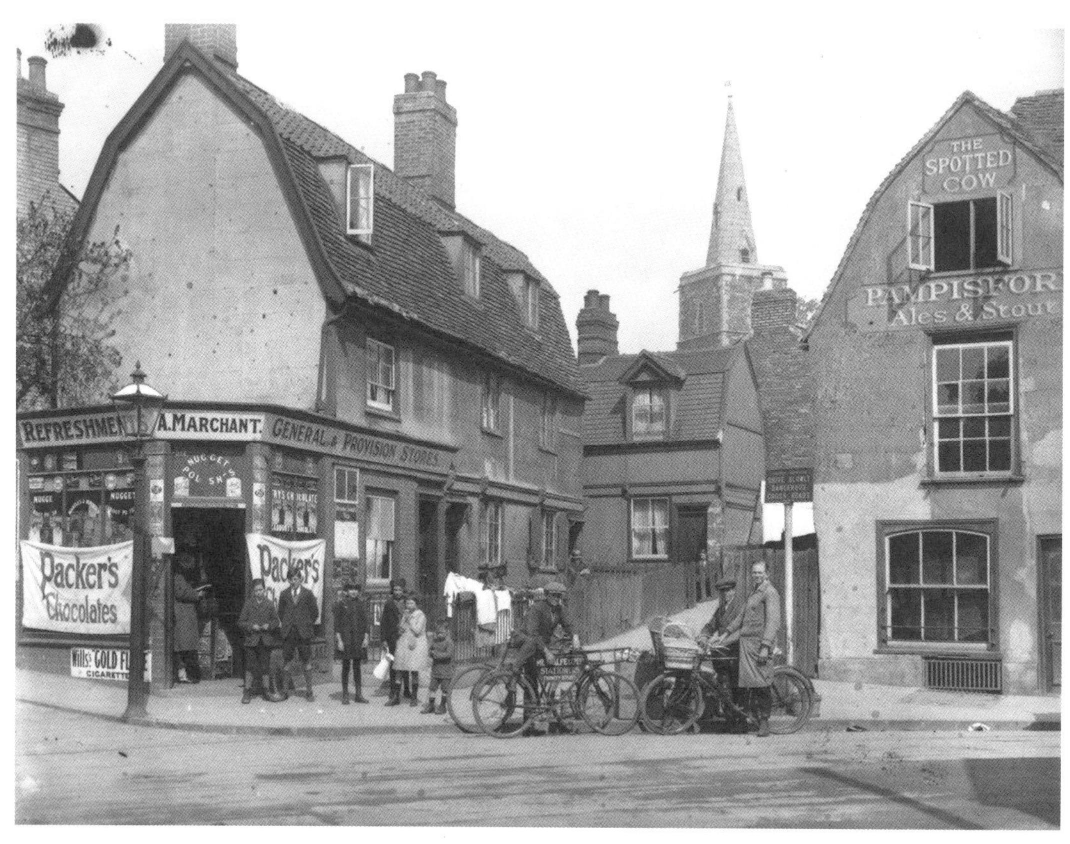

Junction of Northampton Street and Honey Hill looking across what is now the green outside Kettle's Yard, 1920s

A HISTORY OF KETTLE'S YARD

The area known as Kettle's Yard derived its name from the Kettle family, with connections to the site dating back to the eleventh century. In the eighteenth century, the family built a popular theatre on the site, but this was promptly closed by the University of Cambridge authorities on the grounds that it would corrupt the morals of the students. Kettle's Yard gradually declined, becoming one of Cambridge's poorest areas. By the early twentieth century, it was a place for small businesses and jobbing tradespeople, crowded with cottages, workshops, pubs and shops. After the second world war, the national drive for urban reconstruction led to radical change. The lack of investment in the area over the preceding decades had resulted in poorly maintained buildings, which were now being replaced. When new housing for elderly residents was built on Honey Hill, only the four dilapidated cottages that would become Kettle's Yard were spared, saved through the efforts of the Cambridge Preservation Society, but still derelict when Jim and Helen Ede first visited the site in 1956.

'A FRIEND TO ARTISTS'

H.S. (known as 'Jim') Ede (1895–1990) was born in Penarth, near Cardiff; the son of solicitor Edward Hornby Ede and schoolteacher Mildred Ede (née Blanch). He was interested in art and ideas of beauty from a young age. In 1908, aged 13, he spent a year with a family in France, visiting Paris museums and discovering what he later described as an 'elegance of living'. Jim Ede regularly visited the art collections of the Fitzwilliam Museum while he was a boarder at the Leys School in Cambridge (1909–12) and he went on to study at art schools in Cornwall and Edinburgh. At the outbreak of the first world war, Jim Ede enlisted, joining the South Wales Borderers. In 1916, he was sent back from the front with physical and mental exhaustion. His wartime experiences seemed to have shaped his life insofar as he frequently sought to create sanctuaries for art and people – expressed most completely through the making of Kettle's Yard.

Following time spent training officer cadets at Trinity College, Cambridge 1916–17, in November 1917 Jim Ede departed for India from Devonport, Plymouth to serve with the Second Battalion of the 34th Sikh Pioneers. He spent a total of fourteen months in India, in Sialkot (now Pakistan) and Kashmir. Jim Ede would later describe this time as a formative cultural and spiritual experience. After the war, he studied at the Slade School of Fine Art in London, with his fees paid for by an Ex-Service Grant. He developed a keen interest in early Italian Renaissance art and hoped to become a painter.

In January 1921, Jim Ede married Helen Schlapp (1894-1977), the daughter of Otto Schlapp, Professor of German at Edinburgh University, and Anna Schlapp, a musician. The couple first met in 1910, when they were both students at Edinburgh College of Art. While Helene, as she was then, continued her art school education, Jim enlisted in the army. She studied drawing, colour, anatomy, painting, and history and technique - earning a Drawing and Painting Diploma in June 1917. After the war, Jim proposed and Helen (having dropped the 'e' at the end of her name) eventually accepted. They moved into a house in Hampstead Garden Suburb, London. Needing to earn a living, in 1921 Jim Ede took a role as a Photographic Assistant at the National Gallery. In 1922, he became Second Assistant at the National Gallery of British Art (commonly known as Tate Gallery and officially renamed so in 1932). There he supported the Director, Charles Aitken (1869-1936) and began to work with contemporary art and artists, later rising to become Assistant Keeper. The Edes had two daughters Elisabeth, born 18 November 1921, and Mary, born 18 August 1924.

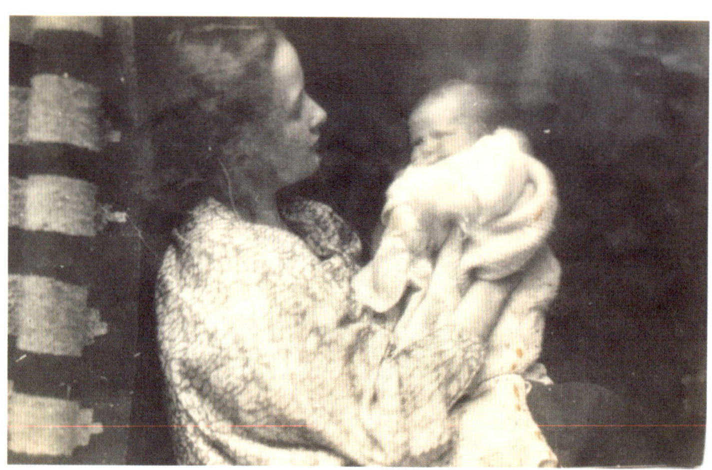

Helen Ede with daughter Mary in Hampstead against the Biskra curtain now at Kettle's Yard, 1924

In April 1925, the family moved to a much larger house, 1 Elm Row in Hampstead, London, where they hosted weekly 'at homes' on Sunday afternoons. During the 1920s the Edes became close friends with artists including Ben and Winifred Nicholson, Christopher Wood, David Jones and Abani Roy. Among those who signed their Hampstead visitors book were artists Vanessa Bell, Georges Braque, Frank Dobson, Sophie Fedorovitch, Naum Gabo, Paul Gangolf, Duncan Grant, Barbara Hepworth, Ivon Hitchens, Frances Hodgkins, Len Lye, Henry Moore, Lászlò Moholy-Nagy, Cedric Morris, Paul Nash, John Skeaping and Edward Wolfe. As well as artists, other visitors included the architect Walter Gropius; collectors George Eumorfopoulos and Margaret Gardiner; writers John Betjeman, Lord David Cecil, David Garnett, Herbert Read, Peter Quennel and Adrian Stokes; composers Arthur Bliss and Constant Lambert; dancers Serge Lifar, Lydia Lopokova and Vaslav Nijinsky; patrons Dorothy and Leonard Elmhirst and Lady Ottoline Morrell; and the actor John Gielgud. Trips to Paris on official Tate Gallery business led to meetings with artists Pablo Picasso, Marc Chagall, Joan Miró and Constantin Brâncuși. In Amsterdam in 1923, Jim Ede met Johanna Bonger, the widow of Vincent van Gogh's brother Theo. He tried to purchase works by Van Gogh for the Tate Gallery, but his colleagues were not so enthusiastic.

These encounters with artists and their studios informed Jim Ede's understanding of art and the significance of its arrangement within a space. Constantin Brâncuși's studio had a particular impact, as did that of Barbara Hepworth, a space she shared with Ben Nicholson from 1932. In later years, Jim Ede acknowledged the central role his friendships with artists played in his career and described himself first and foremost as 'a friend to artists'.

Instrumental to Jim Ede's burgeoning reputation as an authority and collector of modern art was his acquisition, in 1927, of the contents of almost the entire estate of the French-born, but largely London-based, sculptor Henri Gaudier-Brzeska. By the age of twenty-three, Gaudier-Brzeska had made approximately 2,000 works on paper and 115 sculptures. He moved to London from Paris in 1911 but was killed serving in the French army in 1915. His partner, the Polish-born writer Sophie Gaudier-Brzeska (1872–1925) sought to secure his reputation, preserving the estate and helping to arrange a memorial exhibition. She died in 1925 without leaving a will, and in 1927 Jim Ede managed to acquire the majority of the Gaudier-Brzeskas' estates through an intermediary. In 1930 he published a biography of Henri Gaudier-Brzeska that drew heavily on the artist's correspondence with Sophie. The book was republished in 1931 as *Savage Messiah* and became a best-seller in Britain and the United States. It remains a fundamental text for anyone interested in studying the artist. Jim Ede later helped to establish Gaudier-Brzeska's international reputation by supporting exhibitions and donating works to public collections in Britain and France. At the same time, the Tate Gallery was reticent in embracing modern forms of painting and sculpture, and Jim Ede's unofficial role as the gallery's first modern art curator was at odds with the more conservative outlook of the leadership. With an unremitting workload causing a negative impact on his health, in 1936 Ede resigned from both his post at the Tate Gallery and his role as secretary of the Contemporary Art Society. With his family, Ede moved to Tangier, Morocco, beginning a very early professional 'retirement' at the age of forty-one. Employing a local architect, the Edes built a large house a few miles from the centre of the city. It was designed in the international modernist style and named Whitestone. Jim Ede described, 'I thought we had never enjoyed a house so much as we did during those first months [in Tangier]. Our room was large. It had a floor of polished black tiles and four large French windows opening onto a terrace [...] Beyond the land sloped away to the sea and to range after range of mountains.'

Jim Ede planned and undertook two successful art lecture tours across the USA 1937–38 and in early 1939. They supplemented his income from *Savage Messiah* and other occasional writing commissions. When war broke out in September 1939, the Edes initially stayed in Tangier. Through their close friends Alvary Gascoigne (the British Consul-General in Tangier from 1939) and his wife Lorna, the Edes began to invite servicemen into the country on their three days of leave from the garrison in nearby Gibraltar, hosting meals at Whitestone. When Italy joined the war in June 1940, the visits from Gibraltar stopped, and later that year, the Edes shut up their house and left for the USA. When they eventually returned to Tangier in 1945, they substantially altered Whitestone to create a self-contained floor with five bedrooms, allowing them to start a new project: inviting groups of servicemen from Gibraltar to stay for long weekends.

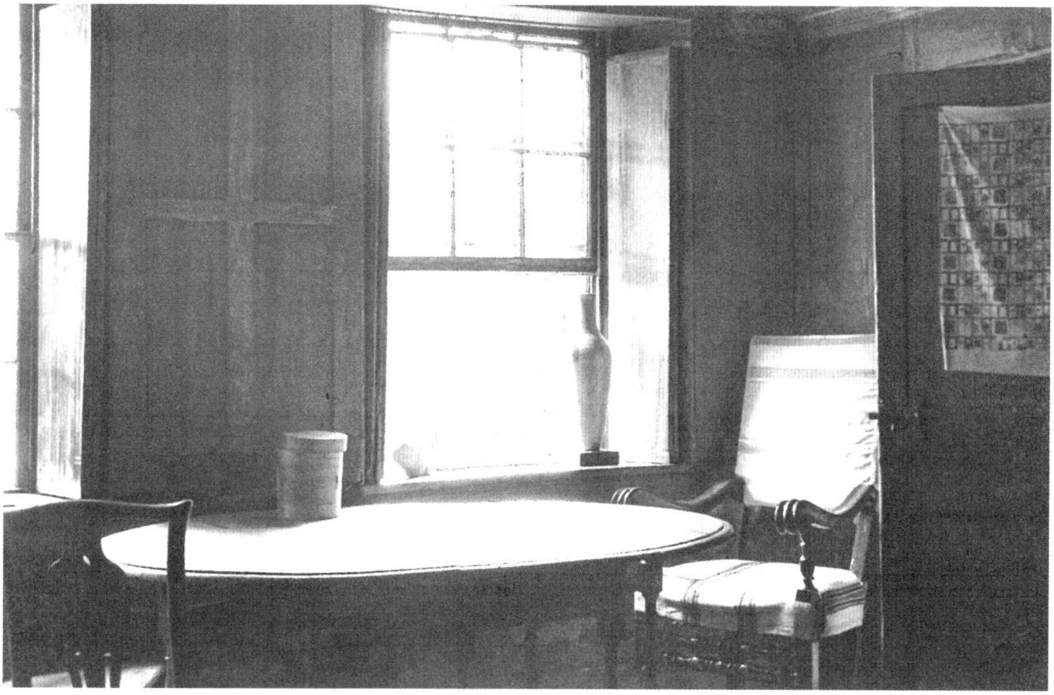

Interior of 1 Elm Row, c. 1930 with works by Henri Gaudier-Brzeska, William Staite Murray and Ben Nicholson, and items of furniture, many of which are now at Kettle's Yard

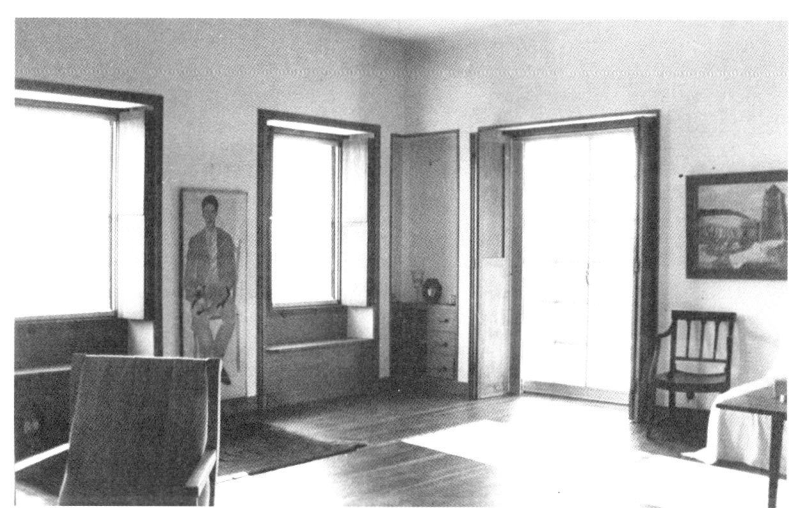

Interior of Whitestone, c. 1937 with paintings by Christopher Wood now at Kettle's Yard

In the US, Jim Ede became friends with artists whose work he went on to collect, including Richard Pousette-Dart. He also met William Congdon, with whom he kept up an affectionate, mostly long-distance, correspondence. Jim Ede maintained a handful of intimate correspondences with men for periods throughout his life – among them the writer T.E. Lawrence and the artist Ian Fairweather. In the early-1950s, the Edes decided to move closer to home. They relocated first to the Loire Valley in France, to a house called Les Charlottières, where they lived between 1952 and 1956, and then finally to England. Helen Ede looked forward to being closer to her children and other family members. For Jim Ede, the need to find a permanent home for his collection of art was paramount.

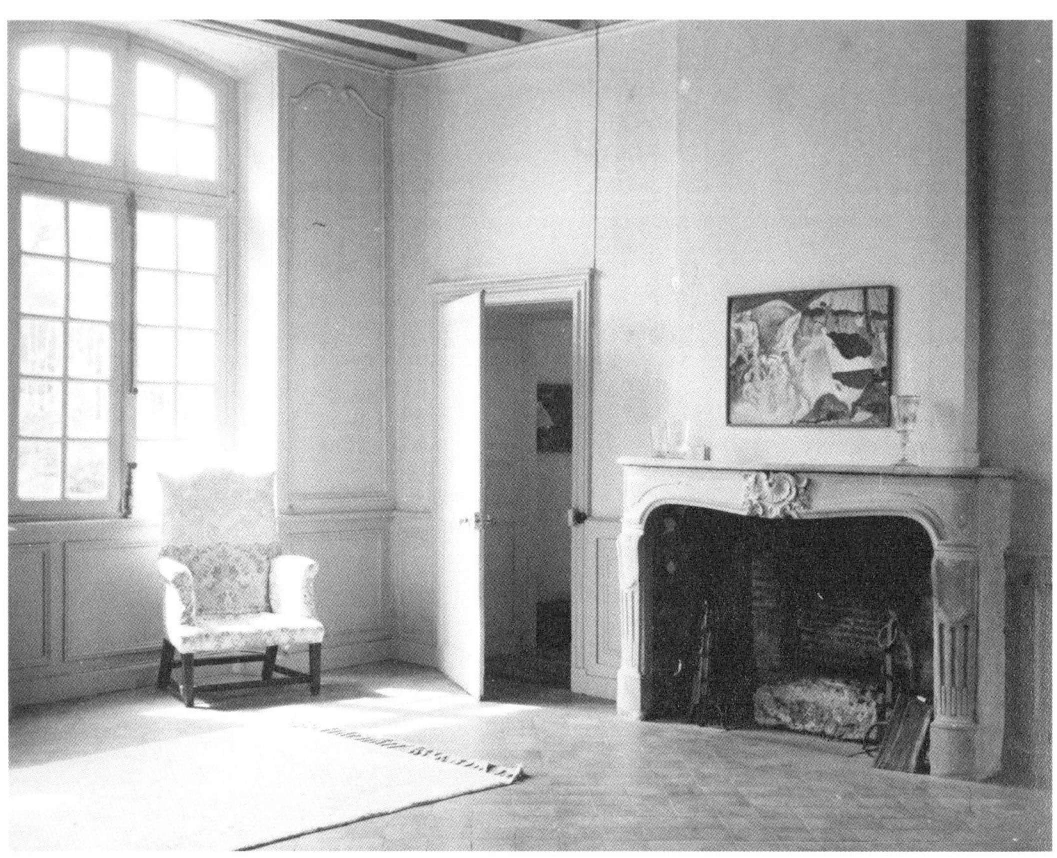

The Edes house at Les Charlottières, France with Christopher Wood's *Ulysses and the Sirens*, 1929

KETTLE'S YARD 1957–73

In a 1956 letter to artist David Jones, Jim Ede wrote:

> It would be interesting to be lent a great house on the verge of a city - or a place of beauty in a town (Cambridge I have in mind) and make it all that I could of lived in beauty, each room an atmosphere of quiet and simple charm, and open to the public (in Cambridge to students especially) and for such a living creation I would give all that I have in pictures and lovely objects, would bear the initial cost of making the house suitable, give my services for the next 10 years [...] Helen and I would live in a bit of it. The rest would look lived in, and its special feature would be I think one of simplicity and loved qualities. There could be a library there (art perhaps) and there could be evenings of chamber music.

In Jim Ede's vision, this house was to be:

> a living place where works of art would be enjoyed, inherent to the domestic setting, where young people could be at home unhampered by the greater austerity of the museum or public art gallery, and where an informality might infuse an underlying formality.

The Edes' search for a suitable home began. They could not find an existing 'great house' in Cambridge and instead, in 1956, settled on a project to transform four derelict cottages in 'Kettle's Yard'. With the help of local architect Rowland De Winton Aldridge, the Edes restored and remodelled the existing early nineteenth-century cottages and, in 1957, moved in.

At Kettle's Yard, Jim Ede installed his collection of art, furniture, glass, ceramics and other objects gathered throughout his lifetime. By carefully considering the precise position of each work of art and object, and their relationship with each other, he aimed to create a perfectly balanced whole, which would become a work of art in its own right. The notion of balance was central to Jim Ede's vision and informed his radical approach to found objects. He created a democracy of display, where everything is attributed equal visual importance. In 1984, he noted that 'pebbles are as important as anything else'.

Concerts were a significant part of Kettle's Yard from the beginning, reflecting Helen Ede's own talent and upbringing as part of a musical family. Her brothers Robin played the cello and Walter the violin. Helen Ede played the piano, and initially those invited to perform at Kettle's Yard used her Bechstein piano in the sitting room on the first floor.

The Edes did not have a fortune at their disposal with which to purchase art. Instead, Jim Ede often acquired works by exchange or through the generosity of his artist friends. He also purchased works by artists who were in the early stages of their careers and had not established themselves in the art market. The Edes' collection is one of outstanding quality and importance. As well as the Gaudier-Brzeska estate, which forms the backbone of the collection, it contains the most substantial publicly accessible holdings of early paintings by Ben Nicholson, Winifred Nicholson and Christopher Wood. Moreover, the display of the Edes' collection of Alfred Wallis paintings helped to establish the painter's place in the history of art. Artists who the Edes came to collect after returning to England include Kate Nicholson (daughter of Ben and Winifred), Simon Nicholson (son of Ben and Barbara Hepworth) and Avinash Chandra.

For the Edes, the practice of opening their home and engaging with new visitors, whatever their background, had begun in Hampstead and continued in Tangier. In Cambridge, it was primarily University undergraduates who visited, and Jim Ede hoped to engage them with the arts no matter what subject they were studying. Through his considerable experience as a touring lecturer, he had developed the notion that each visitor could bring new life to the collection, thus also enhancing his own appreciation of it. In addition to students, the newly opened house soon began to attract artists working locally, such as Cecil Collins and Elisabeth Vellacott, who remembered that:

> When Jim first arrived in Cambridge few people, except for the small group of artists living here, were aware that they lacked any place where they could see and enjoy contemporary twentieth-century art. The Fitzwilliam were not concerned. Jim was a beam of light to us.

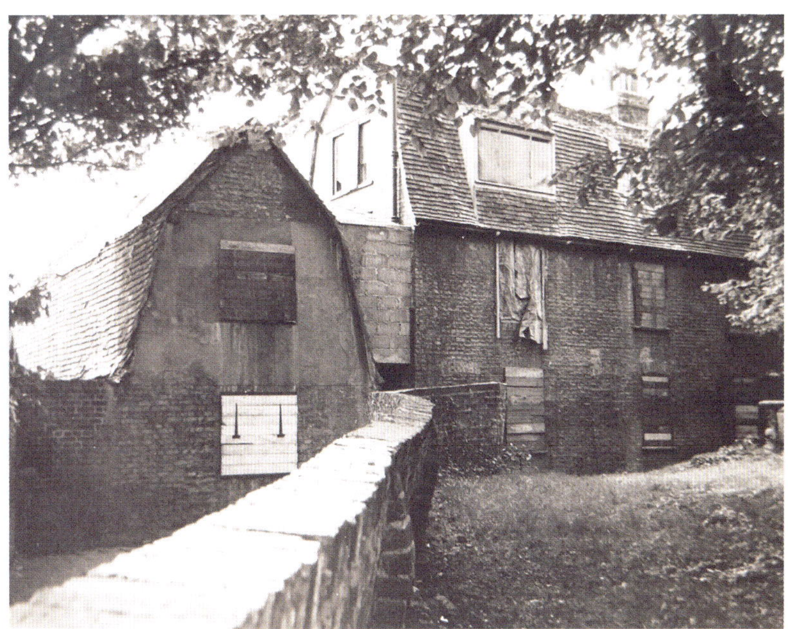

Kettle's Yard, Cambridge, September 1957

Partly as a consequence of Helen Ede's poor health, the daily routine and organisation of the house fell largely to Jim Ede. This pleased him, because it gave him direct control over the realisation of his vision of art in a domestic setting. The tasks of cleaning the house and re-positioning objects became a form of ritual with almost transcendental implications. He recalled that:

> Even the so-called chores I turn to joy; the sweeping of a floor, dust slanting in rays of light, the quality of wood or stone, the cleaning of a window, that thrilling, insubstantial substance glass, hard against driven rain, yet liquid to light.

Jim Ede's sense of the sacred in daily routines, complemented his vision of art as a means toward spiritual growth. Since the early 1920s, he had been deeply engaged with the spiritual and read numerous religious and faith texts. His interest in Christianity was enhanced by his friendship with the painter and poet David Jones, who converted to Catholicism in 1921, and with the painter William Congdon, who became Catholic in 1959. Jim Ede was baptised and confirmed as an Anglican at St Bene't's Church, Cambridge, in 1959.

The Edes officially handed over Kettle's Yard to the University of Cambridge on 30 November 1966. The University assumed responsibility for the building and the collection, but the couple continued to live there, and Jim Ede was given the title of 'honorary curator'. Initially the gift of the collection to the University made little difference to the daily routine. But it soon became apparent that the house needed an extension. Space was required for the growing collection, to meet the Edes' wish that music should play an important role in Kettle's Yard's life, and to accommodate temporary art exhibitions. An avid correspondent, Jim Ede spent much of the late 1960s writing letters to individuals he hoped would help fund the project.

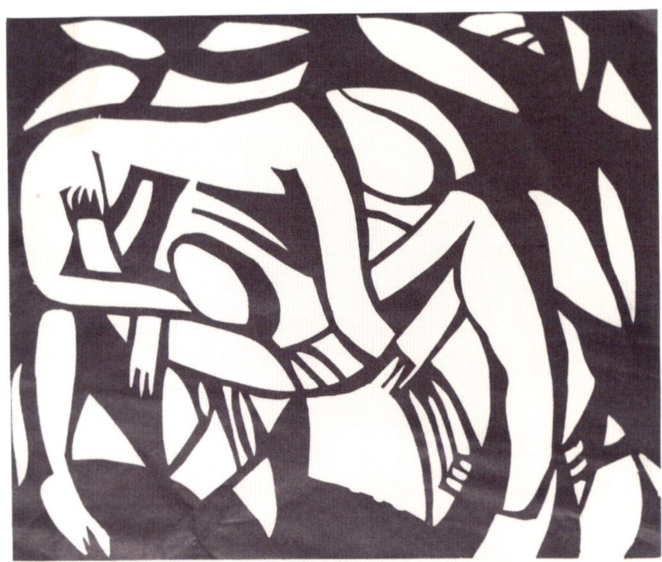

Keith Moffat, poster for Kettle's Yard, 1966

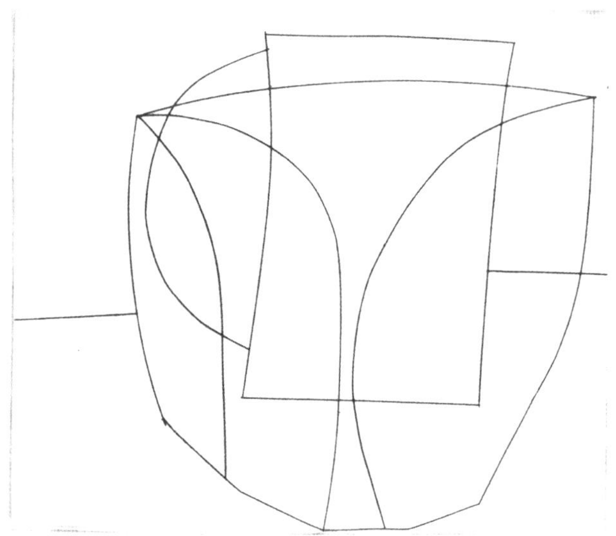

KETTLE'S YARD
UNIVERSITY OF CAMBRIDGE 2/6

Cover of the 1968 catalogue of the Kettle's Yard collection, edited for Granta and the Kettle's Yard Committee by Keith Moffat, featuring Ben Nicholson, *Sexagonal*, 1967

The house extension that resulted was designed by architects Sir Leslie Martin and David Owers, and opened on 5 May 1970 with a concert by the world-renowned musicians Jacqueline du Pré and Daniel Barenboim. It represents an architectural materialisation of Jim Ede's interest in natural light and its ever-changing interplay with objects and spaces, and was created to counterbalance the more intimate conditions of the four original cottages, while sharing their domestic atmosphere. It demonstrated how modernist architecture can be successfully and sympathetically joined to a historic building with reciprocal aesthetic and functional benefits. After the opening of the extension in 1970, the Edes stipulated that there should be 'at least three good concerts a year' in the new larger spaces where 160 people could be comfortably seated to listen to a performance.

When the extension opened, two things became clear: the breadth of the Edes' collection, and its scale, something known only to close friends beforehand. Jim Ede had resumed active collecting in the late 1950s, after a gap of some twenty years. He concentrated on the work of younger artists such as Roger Hilton, William Scott and Italo Valenti – whose collages he acquired from *Documenta III* in 1964. The new extension, however, added to the daily tasks required to keep Kettle's Yard in a presentable state, and now, in his mid-seventies, Jim Ede began to call on student and volunteer help. Helen Ede's worsening health made it difficult for her to bear the daily pressure of visitors. In 1973, the Edes left Kettle's Yard entirely in the hands of the University and moved to Edinburgh, where Helen Ede died four years later. Jim Ede spent his last years as a visitor to hospice residents in the city, before his death in March 1990.

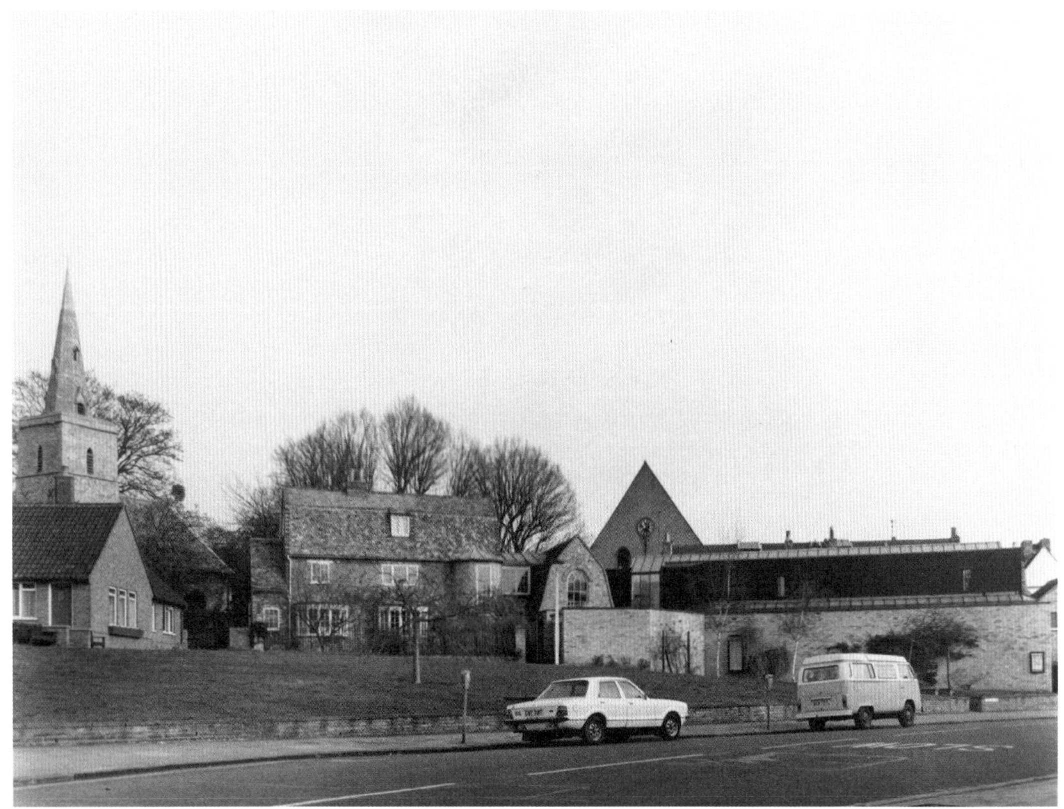

Kettle's Yard, Cambridge, early 1970s

KETTLE'S YARD 1973 – TODAY

The story of Kettle's Yard after the Edes' departure is one of gradual transformation. The gallery adjoining the house, which was built as part of the 1970 extension, was enlarged twice in the 1980s and a third time in 1993-94. This process enabled the development of an ambitious programme of modern and contemporary art exhibitions and educational initiatives, many of which built upon the strengths of the house and collection. Jeremy Lewison organised exhibitions of the work of Ben Nicholson and Henri Gaudier-Brzeska (both 1983) and around constructivism in Britain (1982) and Poland (1984). Hilary Gresty organised shows of the work of Nan Youngman and by artists participating in the programme of residencies at Kettle's Yard, as well as innovative group shows such as *After 1789: Ideas and Images of Revolution* (1989). Under the directorship of Michael Harrison, artists were also invited to exhibit in the house, as in the 1995 exhibition *Open House* that featured works by Judith Goddard and Catherine Yass. In 2004, Jamie Fobert Architects were commissioned by Harrison to begin work on a new education wing. This project was extended by the succeeding director Andrew Nairne, to encompass new galleries and a welcome area, opened in 2018.

While Jim Ede stipulated that Kettle's Yard should 'grow and change only very slowly', during the period in which the Edes lived at Kettle's Yard, he would frequently move and exchange the artworks on display. The opening of the extension of the house in 1970 necessitated bringing many works across from the attic rooms to hang in the new building, resulting in the conversion of this space into one primarily dedicated to the work of Henri Gaudier-Brzeska.

Jim Ede kept in very close touch with Kettle's Yard despite the couple's retirement to Edinburgh in 1973; he expected the new curators to share his level of commitment, and in one letter to an applicant for the post, he described the role as that of 'resident' and stressed the importance of committing oneself to 'make it live' for others. He even sought accounts from volunteers and other friends visiting to monitor the spaces, and while he wrote to Kettle's Yard staff in 1980 to explain that the positions of objects, 'may be altered from time to time', he had earlier passed on 'corrections' to particular placements if works were discovered to have strayed too far from their original positions.

Today, the Edes' 1973 arrangement of the collection within the house is maintained as closely as possible. A handful of new acquisitions were added to the collections displays in 2025, in areas of the house that had already been altered over the years during building work. These additions enable the house to 'grow' a little, some seven decades after Kettle's Yard first opened its doors. They reflect and contribute to the warm reception extended to visitors through exhibition and learning programmes, and ensure that, according to Jim Ede's wishes, 'future generations will still find a home and a welcome, a refuge of peace and order' within the house.

Preserving the Edes' vision would not be possible without generous support from the Friends and Patrons of Kettle's Yard. The house is open six days out of seven, and the music programme established by the Edes has developed to include not only chamber concerts, but contemporary music and student recitals. The Art for Students scheme, through which Jim Ede enabled young people to borrow pictures from his collection to hang in their own university rooms, also continues to run annually, extending the Edes' fundamental belief that art should be part of our everyday experience.

The following guide to the artworks and objects on display in the house features short introductions to each space alongside lists of works with their collection numbers. Those objects collected by the Edes have the suffix 'E', and those collected by the Edes which were part of the permanent displays in the house during their time living at Kettle's Yard have the suffix 'EH'. Those acquired by subsequent curators have no suffix. Occasionally, for reasons of conservation, two works will rotate in one location. In these instances both are listed. Objects not included in the lists are referred to in the brief introductory texts. More information on the artists whose work features prominently at Kettle's Yard and with who the Edes were friends can be found in *Kettle's Yard Art and Artists*, published as a companion to the *Kettle's Yard House Guidebook*.

— Sebastiano Barassi and Inga Fraser

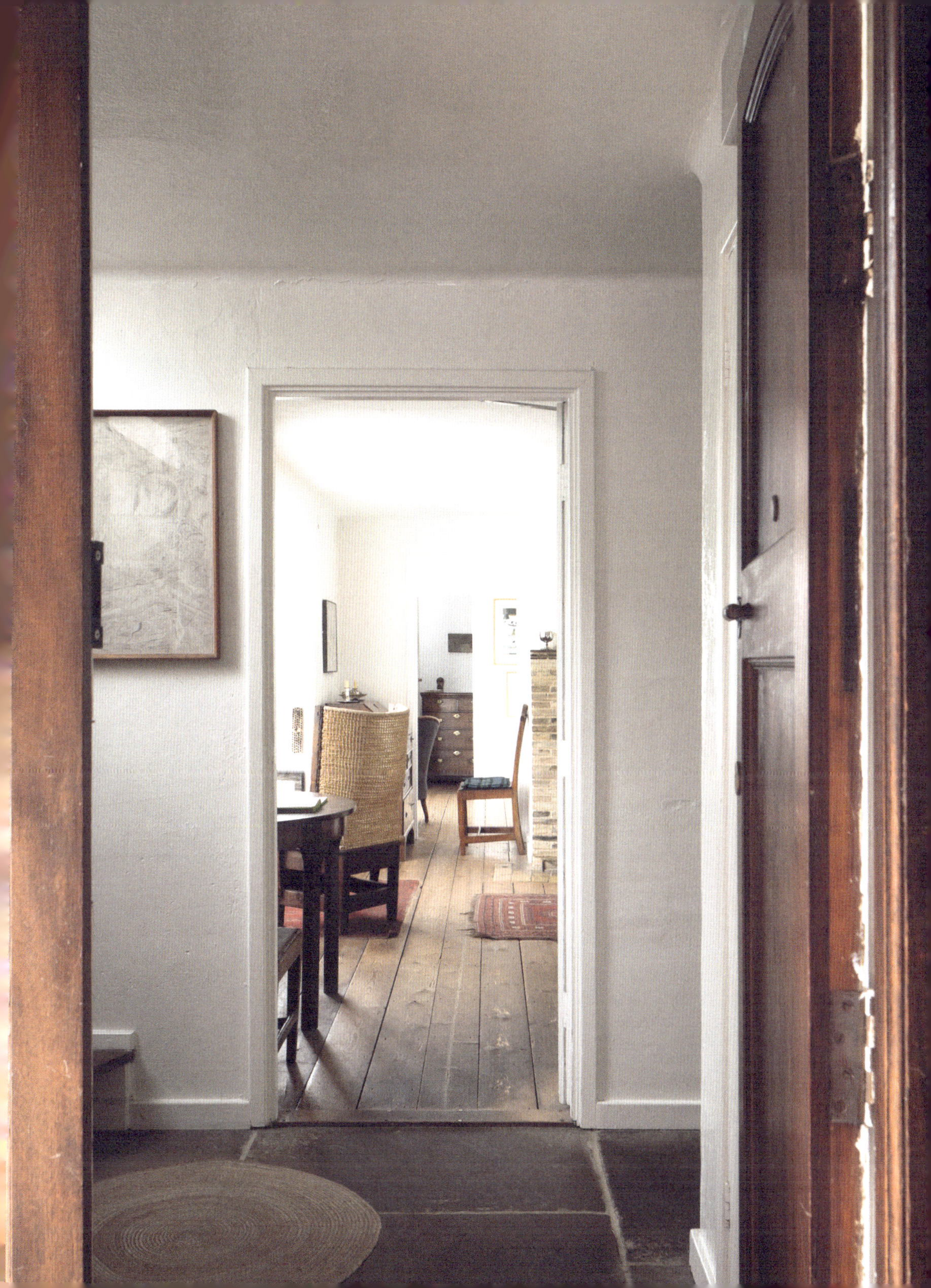

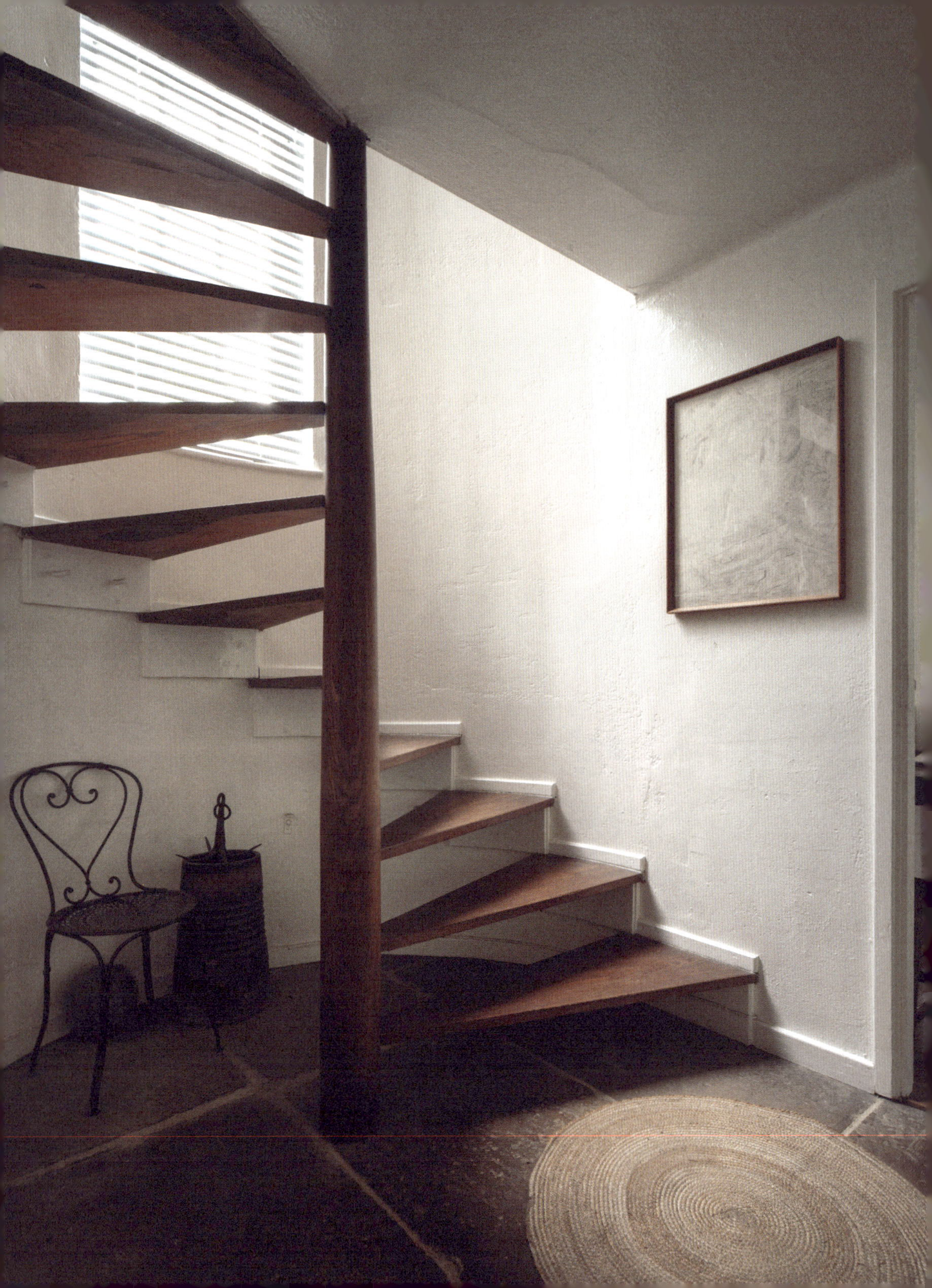

ENTRANCE HALL

After ringing the cork door pull to enter the Kettle's Yard house, visitors make their way into a small entrance area with a stone floor and a circular mat. The eighteenth-century Chippendale mirror was purchased when Jim and Helen Ede married in 1921. The nineteenth-century French wrought iron park chair beneath the spiral staircase was acquired during their time in Tangier. It sits alongside more utilitarian objects: a spherical metal fishing float, a hook and an earthenware chimney pot salvaged from the roof during refurbishment and used as an umbrella stand. Jim Ede ensured there was a painting by Alfred Wallis in every room of the house, and a framed image of a work by David Jones introduces the first of many reproductions and casts at Kettle's Yard.

1 Mirror, England, 18th century
Wood and glass
KY00470.EH

2 Two carved shapes, undated
Wood
KY00013a-b.EH

3 David Jones
The Four Queens, 1941
Offset print on paper
KY00753.EH

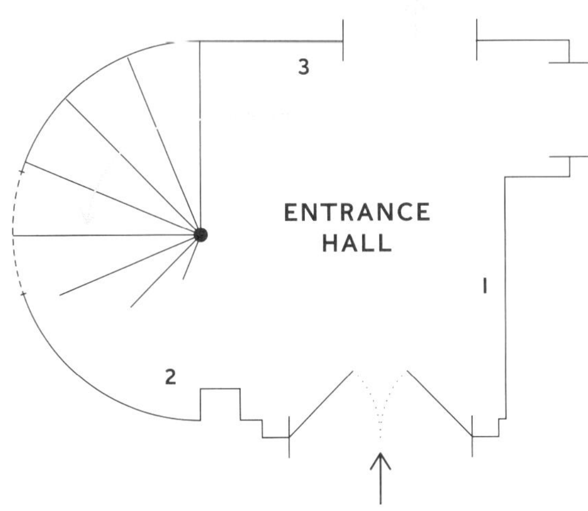

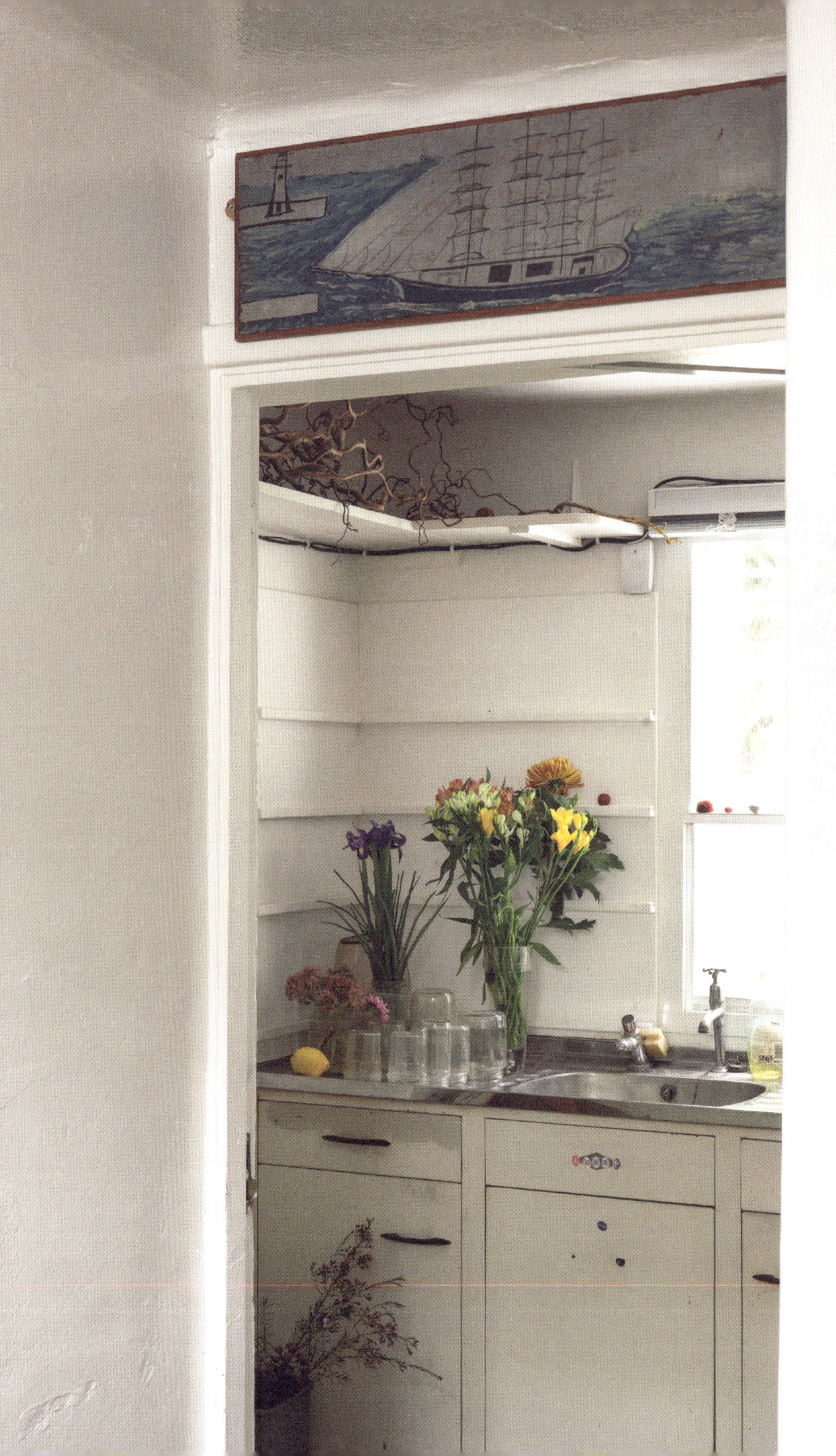

KITCHEN

The kitchen at Kettle's Yard is small but functional. Jim Ede recalled, 'It was, I know, a makeshift kitchen but what is a home without a kitchen, and ours was always in a state to be visited and was almost beautiful and enjoyed by visitors from abroad.' While the Edes lived in the house, the kitchen floor was covered with a 'grey linoleum' and 'had its own pictures'. These were subsequently removed while the space was in use as a break room for visitor assistants. Today, it remains a working space, where fresh flowers for the house are prepared.

1 Alfred Wallis
Four-masted schooner and lighthouse, undated
Oil paint on wood
KY000399.EH

2 Alfred Wallis
Lighthouse and two sailing ships, undated
Oil paint on card
KY00400.EH

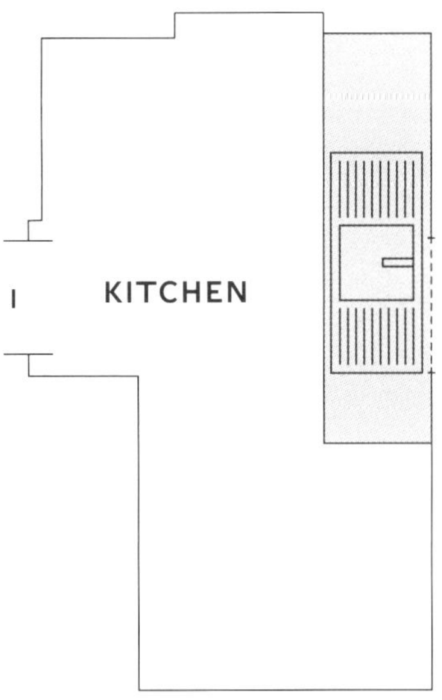

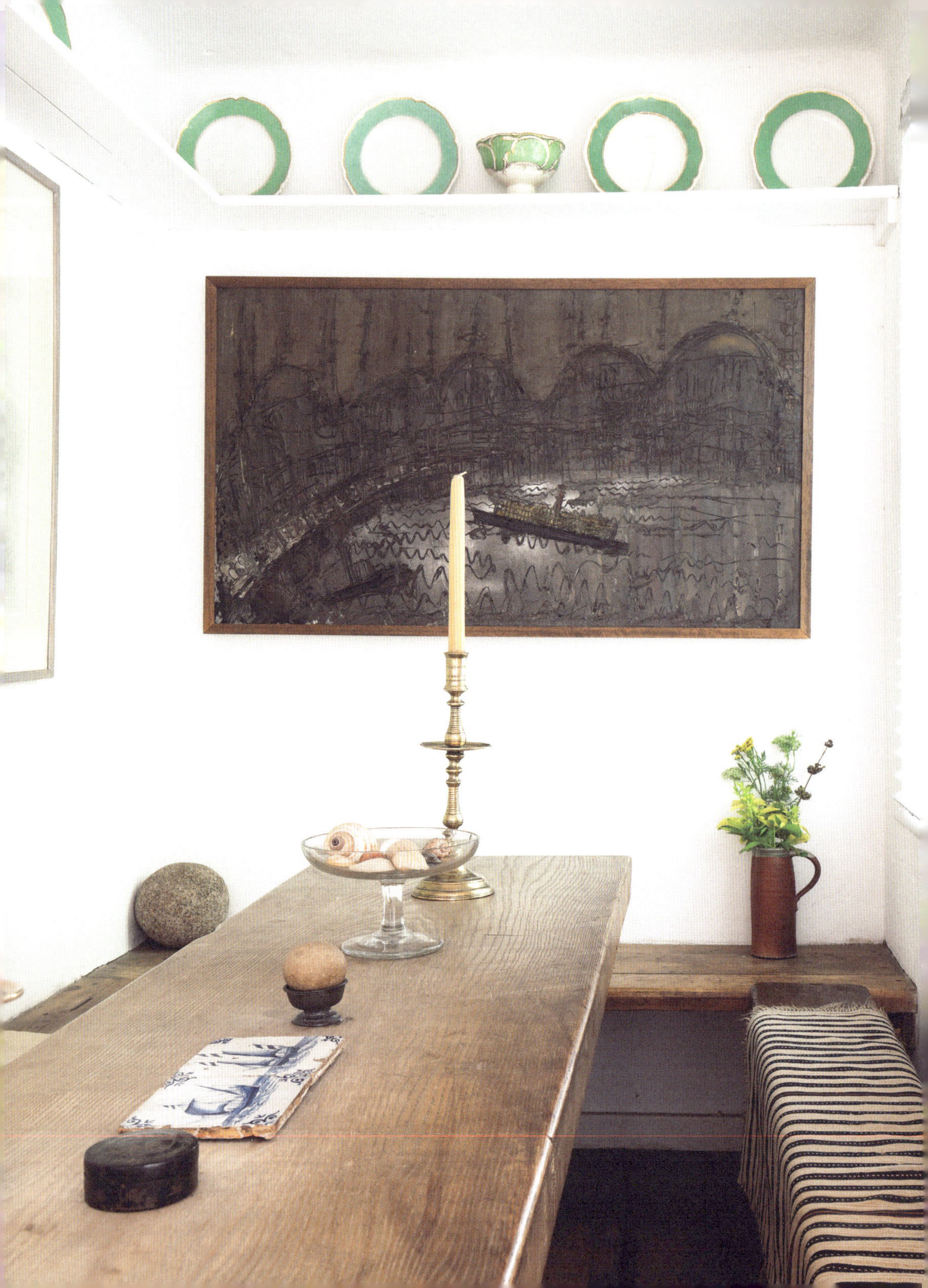

SITTING AND DINING ROOM

The sitting room introduces some of the recurring themes of the Kettle's Yard house. Relationships between art and found objects, contrasts between light and shadow, and smooth and textured surfaces are central to this space. During the original refurbishment of the cottages, bay windows were added in this room and the next, to allow more daylight to enter. The venetian blinds were selected for the effects of light they create upon objects and artworks. The rugs in this space originate from Afghanistan. Because of the inevitable wear and tear with use, they have been replaced over the years. In the first bay window, a green glass fishing float, an ivory billiard ball and a basket of pebbles, graded according to colour, accompany works of art on a table purchased in Morocco, with a crystal necklace on the windowsill.

Fossils, shells, and stones are placed carefully on the fireplace mantelpiece, next to nineteenth-century English silver lustre goblets and elsewhere. The corner shelves hold a collection of turquoise-coloured early twentieth-century Chinese ceramics and a set of mid-nineteenth-century blue and white Staffordshire plates. More utilitarian objects, including an old broom head, jelly moulds, and a lemon (replaced weekly), offer lessons in balance and form. The two brass candlesticks on the narrow dining table were purchased by Jim Ede during visits to Mazagan and Taroudant in Morocco. The glass decanters on top of the tall wooden cider screw once belonged to the novelist George Moore and were given to the Edes by Lady Cunard (Maud Alice Burke). The Edes maintained a guestbook while they lived in the house, placed on the semi-circular table by the door. Today's visitors are invited to sign the current guestbook.

1 Mezcala head,
Mesoamerica,
c. 300–100 BCE
Stone
KY01177.EH

2 David Jones
Seascape from a Terrace, 1929
Watercolour on paper
KY00345.EH

3 Mario Sironi
Landscape, late 1940s
Conté crayon, ink and gouache on paper
KY01019.EH

4 Jarlet, China,
c. 12th century
Glazed stoneware
KY01106.EH

5 Chair, Orkney, Scotland, 1906
Wood and straw
KY00301.EH

6 Ben Nicholson
jug, 1967
Etching on paper
KY00932.EH

7 John Acland
Carving, c. 1960
Slate
KY00791.EH

8 David Peace
Acho ellen Bremblens, 1971
Engraved glass goblet
KY01193.EH

9 Table, Morocco,
20th century
Wood and metal
KY00728.EH

10 Christopher Wood
Flowers, 1930
Oil paint on board
KY00629.EH

11 Chief's seat, Ātiu,
Cook Islands,
undated
Wood
KY00303.EH

12 Decorated pot,
Morocco, c. 1900
Earthenware
KY00735.EH

13 Queen Anne bureau,
England, 18th century
Oak wood and brass
KY00302.EH

14 Christopher Wood
Paris Snow Scene, 1926
Oil paint on canvas
KY00343.EH

15 Dish (with feathers),
Beykoz, Turkey,
19th century
Gilded glass
KY00836.EH

16 Fireplace back,
England, c. 1650
Iron
KY00204.EH

17 Christopher Wood
Ship in Harbour, 1928
Incised wash paint on board
KY00340.EH

18 Elisabeth Vellacott
Trees, Orchard in Spring, 1967
Graphite on paper
KY00805.EH

19 William Congdon
Istanbul no.2, 1953
Oil paint on board
KY00771.EH

20 Handira (shawl),
Ayt Yazza, Morocco,
20th century
Wool
KY00733.EH

21 Two tiles, probably
Delft, Netherlands,
18th century
Tin-glazed earthenware
KY00378a-b.EH

22 Ben Nicholson
1927 (apples and pears), c. 1927
Oil and graphite on canvas
KY00332.EH

23 Christopher Wood
Le Phare, 1930
Oil paint on board
KY00342.EH

24 Alfred Wallis
Seascape-ships sailing past the Longships,
c. 1928
Oil paint on canvas
KY00396.EH

25 Pewter dish, England,
17th century
Metal
KY00150.EH

26 Lubaina Himid
Saving it for Later,
2025
Acrylic paint on interior wall
KY01441

27 Joan Miró
Tic Tic, 1927
Oil paint on canvas
KY00695.EH

28 Waterford decanters,
1820–25
Glass
KY00713.EH

29 Cider press screw,
France,
c. 19th century
Wood
KY00724.EH

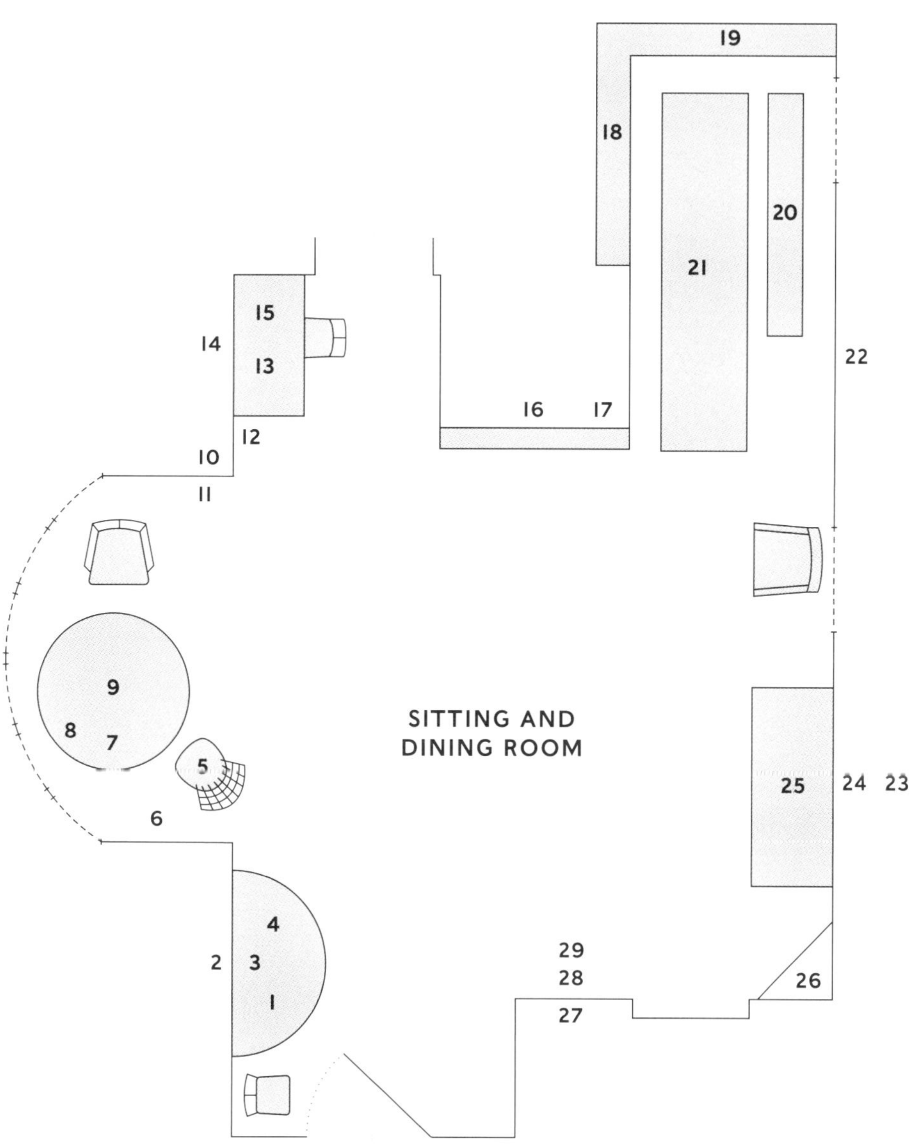
19
18
20
21
15
14
13
22
16
17
12
10
11
9
SITTING AND
DINING ROOM
8
7
5
25
24
23
6
4
2
3
1
29
28
27
26

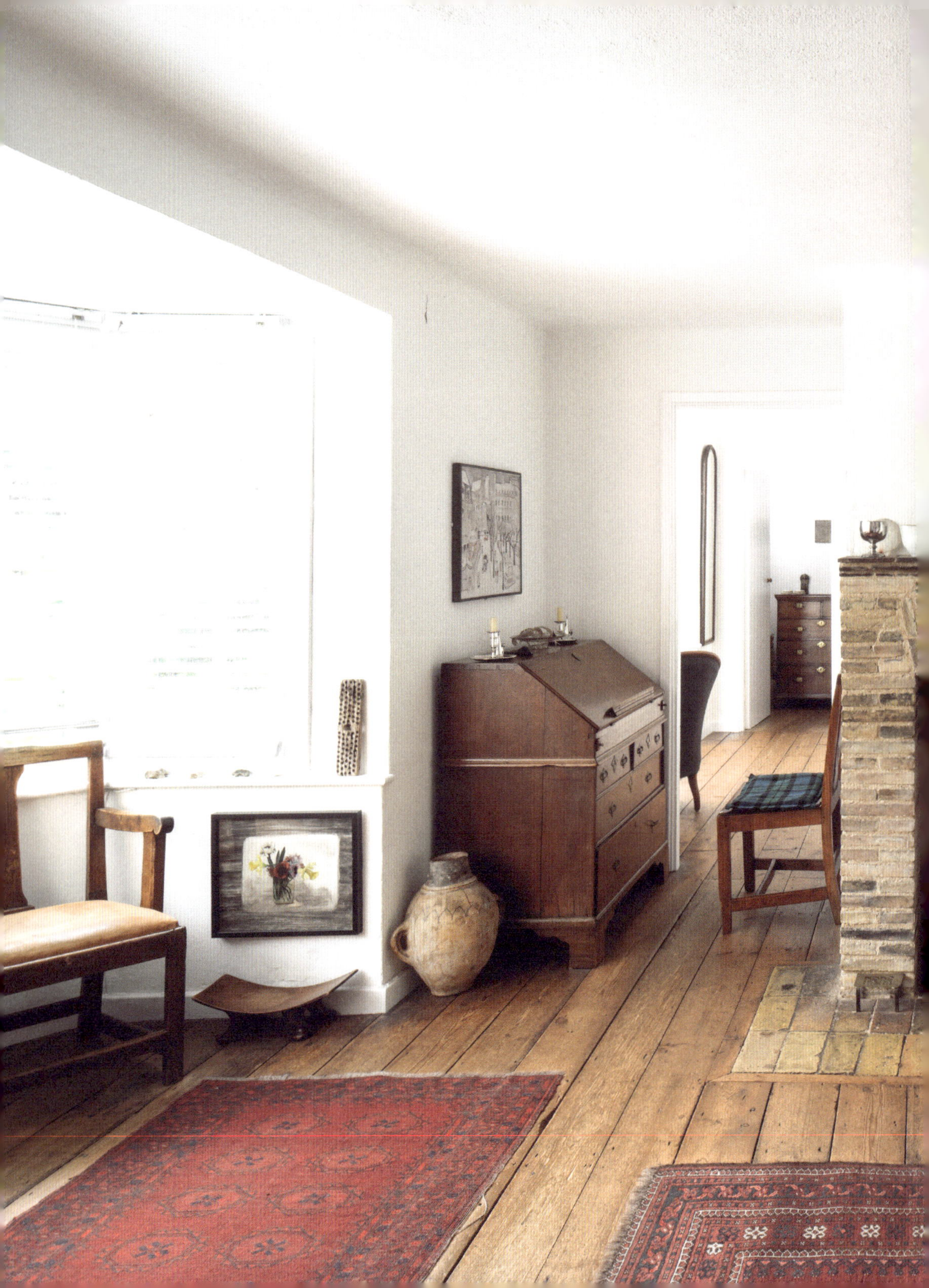

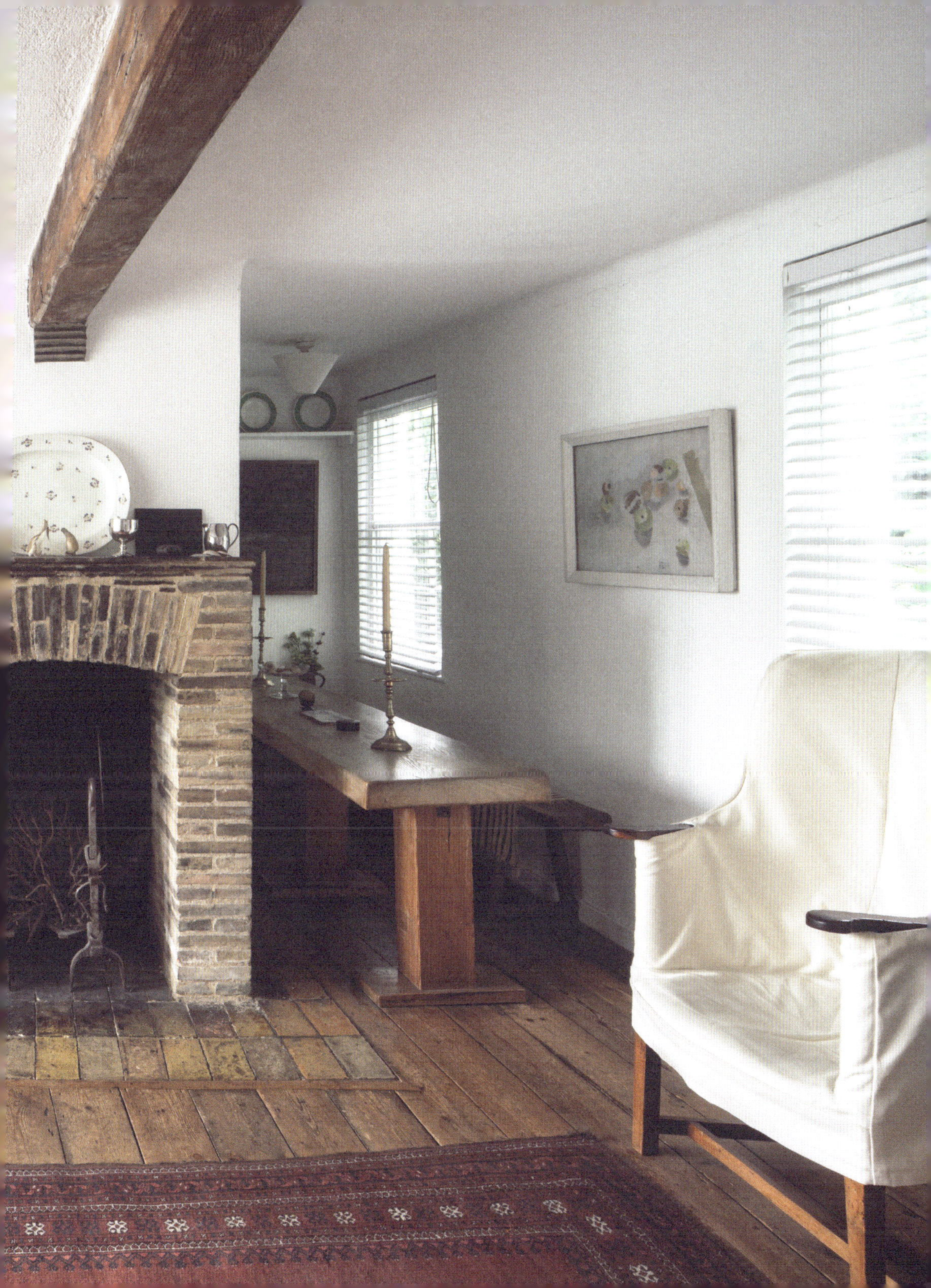

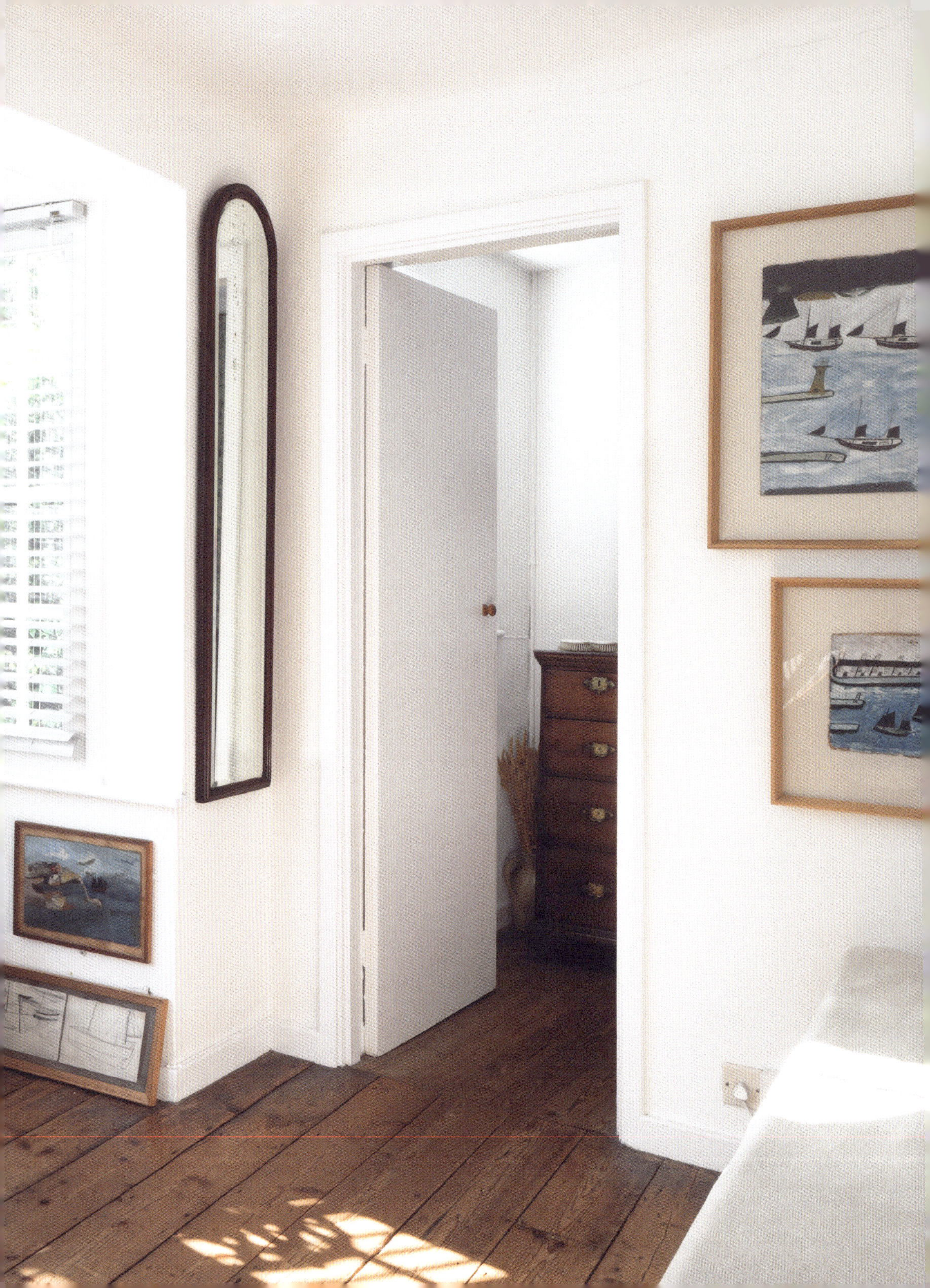

JIM EDE'S BEDROOM AND BATHROOM

Jim Ede's bedroom, just off the sitting room, features a French winged chair and an English Windsor chair placed around a low round cedar table that the Edes purchased while living in Morocco (1936-52). A 1968 cast of Henri Gaudier-Brzeska's *Toy (Torpedo Fish)* sits in a constellation of objects. An upturned cockle shell that was once used for a christening at St. Peter's church next door, is placed near to a green glass fishing float. A closed Rose of Jericho is also placed on the table, often referred to as a 'resurrection plant' because of its capacity to migrate with the wind before unfurling and taking root when it reaches water. The spiral of pebbles was begun by Jim Ede on a seaside holiday in Norfolk in 1958 and remade at Kettle's Yard upon his return. A twisted wire man, made by the Edes' granddaughter Caroline (known as Quince) hangs from the cord of the blind. The bedroom includes works by Ben Nicholson, Alfred Wallis, David Jones, Henry Moore and Henri Gaudier-Brzeska, all artists Jim Ede felt a great affinity with. In the cupboard behind the door are eighteenth, nineteenth and early twentieth-century ceramics from China, England and Japan and stone and bronze versions of Gaudier-Brzeska's *Duck*.

In the bathroom, alongside works by William Congdon, Christopher Wood and a printed textile by Ben Nicholson, is a drawing by the Edes' other granddaughter Jane. Stone flints on top of the oak chest of drawers were chosen by Jim Ede for their likeness to Henry Moore's sculptures.

BEDROOM

1 Ben Nicholson
1934 (relief), 1934
Oil paint, graphite and coloured card
KY00643.EH

2 Caroline 'Quince' Adams
Wire man, called 'Gwllm'
Metal
KY00825.EH

3 Ben Nicholson
sexagonal, 1967
Engraving on paper
KY00926.EH

4 Table, Morocco, 20th century
Wood and metal
KY00729.EH

5 Rose of Jericho, undated
KY00732.EH

6 Henri Gaudier-Brzeska
Torpedo Fish (Toy), 1914 (cast 1968)
Bronze
KY00935.EH

7 Spiral of pebbles, c. 1958
KY00790.EH

8 Ben Nicholson
1952 (goblet), 1952
Engraving, ink, graphite and wash on cardboard
KY00764.EH

9 Ben Nicholson
c. 1928 (Cornish port), c. 1928
Oil paint on card
KY00334.EH

10 Ben Nicholson
1945 (boats in St Ives Harbour), 1945
Graphite on paper
KY00751.EH

11 Alfred Wallis
Five ships (Mount's Bay), c. 1928
Oil paint and graphite on card
KY00404.EH

12 Alfred Wallis
Houses at the water's edge (Porthleven), c. 1925-28
Oil paint and graphite on card
KY00405.EH

13 Henry Moore
Head, 1928
Stone on plaster base
KY00786.EH

14 Ben Nicholson
1941 (abstract), 1941
Gouache on board
KY00754.EH

15 David Jones
Vexilla Regis, 1948
Graphite and watercolour on paper
KY00757.EH

16 Henri Gaudier-Brzeska
Duck, 1914
Serpentine stone
KY00492.EH

17 Henri Gaudier-Brzeska
Duck, 1914 (cast 1964-68)
Bronze
KY00816.EH

BATHROOM

18 Jane Adams
Two girls, one with a doll, 1955
Graphite and crayon on paper
KY00783.EH

19 William Congdon
Moonlight Subiaco, 1967
Graphite on paper
KY00831.EH

20 Henri Gaudier-Brzeska
Door-Knocker, 1914
Carved brass
KY00491.EH

21 William Congdon
Piazza San Marco no. 5
Oil paint on hardboard
KY00773.EH

22 Ben Nicholson
letters and numbers, c. 1933
Linoblock print on cotton
KY00704.EH

23 Christopher Wood
Landscape at Vence, 1927
Oil paint on canvas
KY00614.EH

24 Alfred Wallis
Grey steam boat, undated
Oil paint and graphite on card
KY00412.EH

25 Alfred Wallis
Three masted barque with three small ships, undated
Oil paint on card
KY00406.EH

26 Munnyuure cloth, Mali, 20th century
Cotton
KY00737.EH

27 William Congdon
Guatemala no. 7 (Dying Vulture), 1957
Oil paint on hardboard
KY00998.EH

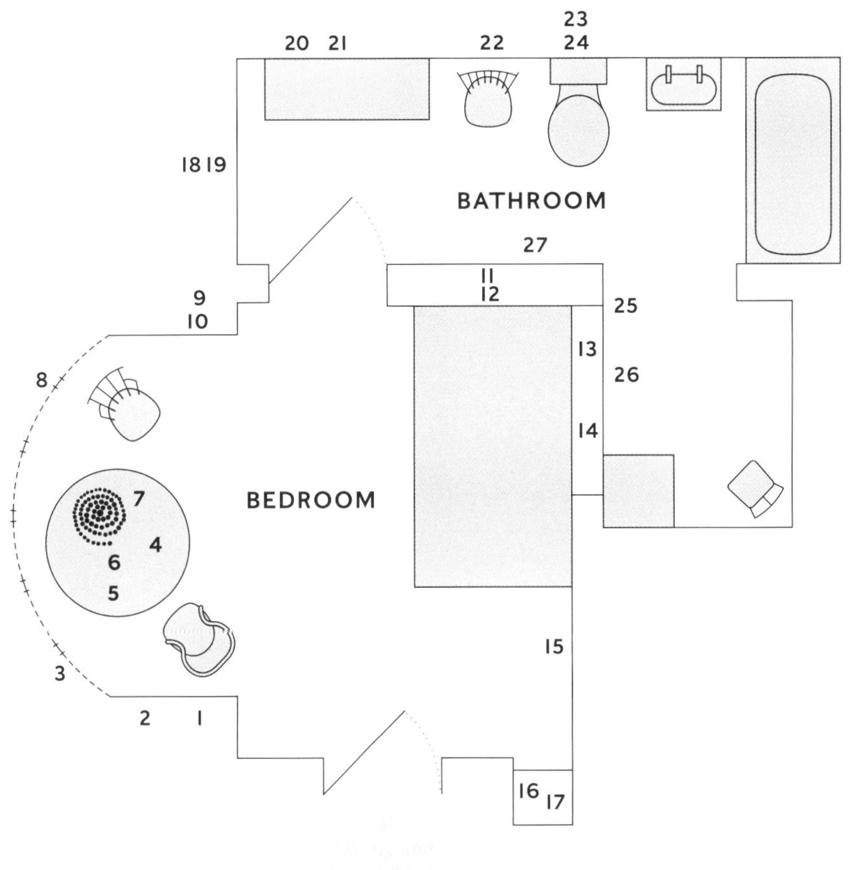

23
20 21 22 24
18 19
BATHROOM
27
11
12
9
10
25
13
26
8
14
7
BEDROOM
4
6
5
15
3
2 1
16 17

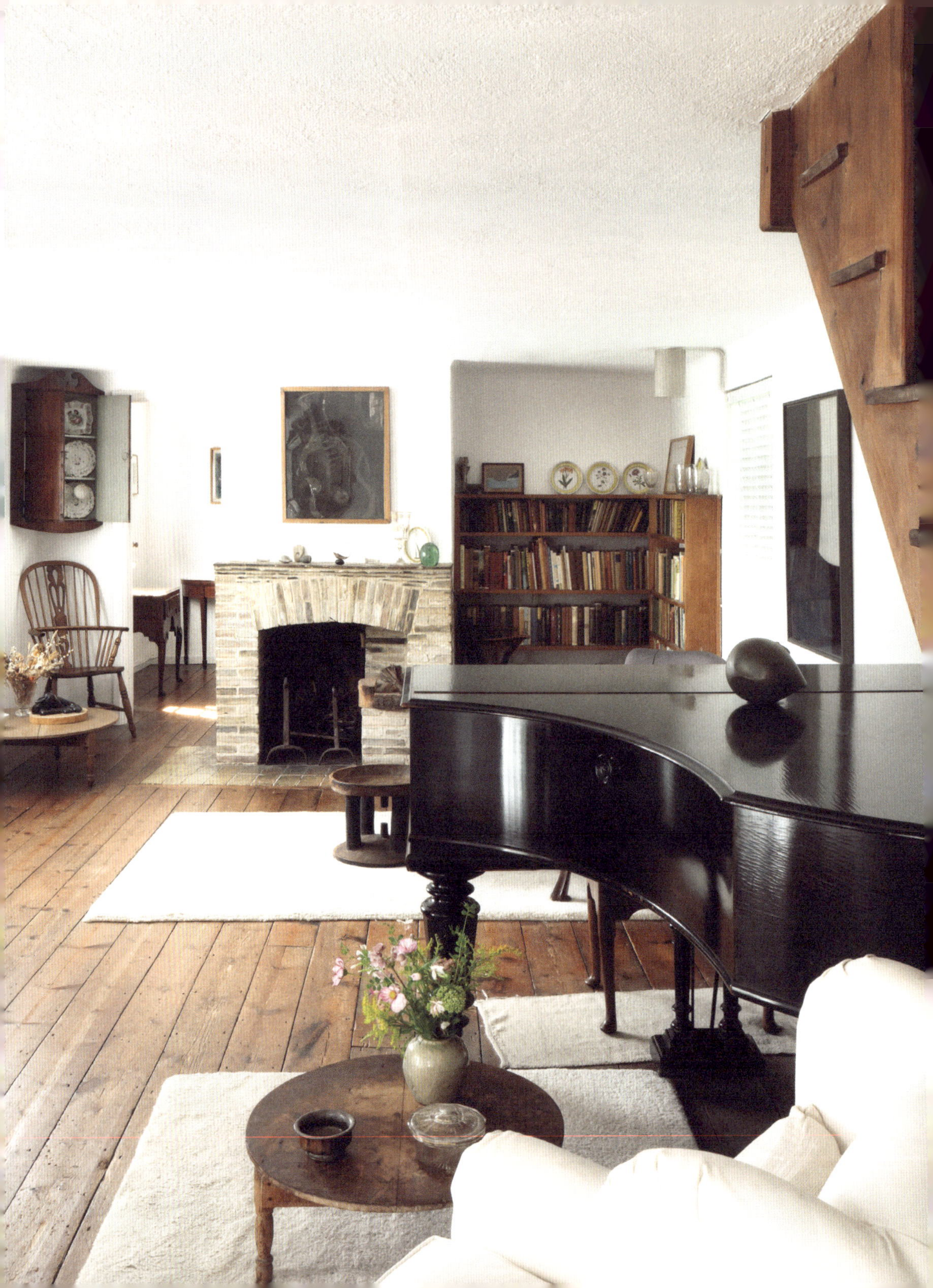

BECHSTEIN ROOM

The Edes added the spiral staircase leading up to the first floor in 1956. Its treads were salvaged from a large house being demolished nearby. An eighteenth-century Venetian mirror, given to the Edes by the collectors Frederick and Gertrude Leverton Harris, welcomes visitors into the room. This more spacious sitting room was primarily Helen Ede's. Her Bechstein piano was used for musical performances in the house, prior to the opening of the extension in 1970. On top of the piano is Constantin Brâncuși's stone cast *Prometheus* and behind is a drawing by the artist which he gave to Jim Ede in 1926. Jim Ede acquired the yak bell by the landing balustrade in India in 1917 while he was serving in the Army during the first world war. The terracotta amphora was made in Safi on Morocco's western coast and acquired while the Edes were living in Tangier. The small table on the rug by the piano is carved from a single piece of wood.

The bookshelves in the corner of this room hold a range of novels and children's books. On top are ringed Coalport plates that Jim Ede (mistakenly) believed to have been decorated by the renowned porcelain painter William 'Quaker' Pegg (1775-1851). Jim Ede originally displayed brass and jade rings made by the artist Richard Pousette-Dart next to the plates, balanced upright to echo their yellow border, but these are now displayed in Helen Ede's bedroom cabinet. On the mantlepiece is a stone Jim Ede thought looked like a sculpture by Barbara Hepworth, and a seed pod he thought resembled a bird, placed on a pebble to look like an egg.

In the mahogany corner cabinet are two nineteenth-century glass decanters made in Bohemia (now part of the Czech Republic) and a collection of nineteenth-century porcelain, including 'New Dresden' patterns, Spode teacups and a pearlware teapot. Below, on another table purchased in Morocco, is a bronze fawn by Henri Gaudier-Brzeska, placed near a bowl by Lucie Rie, a glass vase of dried flowers and an iron barrel ring.

1 Mirror, Venice, Italy, 18th century
Glass
KY00481.EH

2 Lantern, Japan, 19th century
Cloth and wood
R00051

3 Amphora, Morocco, 20th century
Terracotta
KY00736.EH

4 Yak bell and stand, Tibet, 19th century
Wood, metal and leather
KY00304.EH

5 David Jones
Flora in Calix-Light, 1950
Graphite and watercolour on paper
KY00765.EH

6 Stone tools, Pitjantjatjara, South Australia, undated
L00004A-C

7 Italo Valenti
Cervi volanti; Cerfs-volants, 1964
Paper and watercolour on paper
KY00919.EH

8 David Jones
Lourdes, 1928
Watercolour on paper
KY00344.EH

9 Henri Gaudier-Brzeska
Sleeping Fawn, 1913 (cast 1960)
Bronze
KY00814.EH

10 Lucie Rie
Bowl, 1950s
Glazed stoneware
KY01102.E

11 Ben Nicholson
1928 (Banks Head - Cumbrian landscape), 1928
Oil paint on canvas
KY00628.EH

12 Ben Nicholson
1932-33 (guitar), 1932-33
Oil paint on canvas
KY00641.EH

13 'Proboscidea louisianica' or 'Devil's-claw' seed pod and pebble
KY00093.EH

14 Francine Del Pierre
Bowl, 1960s
Terracotta, glazed
KY00933.EH

15 Skull of a crucifix catfish, undated
KY01099.EH

16 Alfred Wallis
Schooner on a blue sea, undated
Oil paint and graphite on card
KY00407.EH

17 Alfred Wallis
Three sailing boats in a line, undated
Oil paint on paper mounted on card
KY00397.EH

18 Roger Hilton
October 1955 Calm (Black, Grey, Brown and White), 1955
Oil paint on canvas
KY00789.EH

19 Table, West Africa, early 20th century
Wood
KY00310.EH

20 Constantin Brâncuși
Nude, c. 1920-25
Pen and ink on paper
KY00480.EH

21 Constantin Brâncuși
Prometheus, 1912
Cast stone
KY00980.EH

22 Tea bowl, Tibet, undated
Metal
KY00085.EH

23 Ben Nicholson
1948 (three pears), 1948
Graphite on paper
KY00752.EH

24 Christmas tree bauble, England, 19th century
Glass
KY00395.EH

25 Laurence Whistler
Untitled, 1974
Window engraving
KY01164

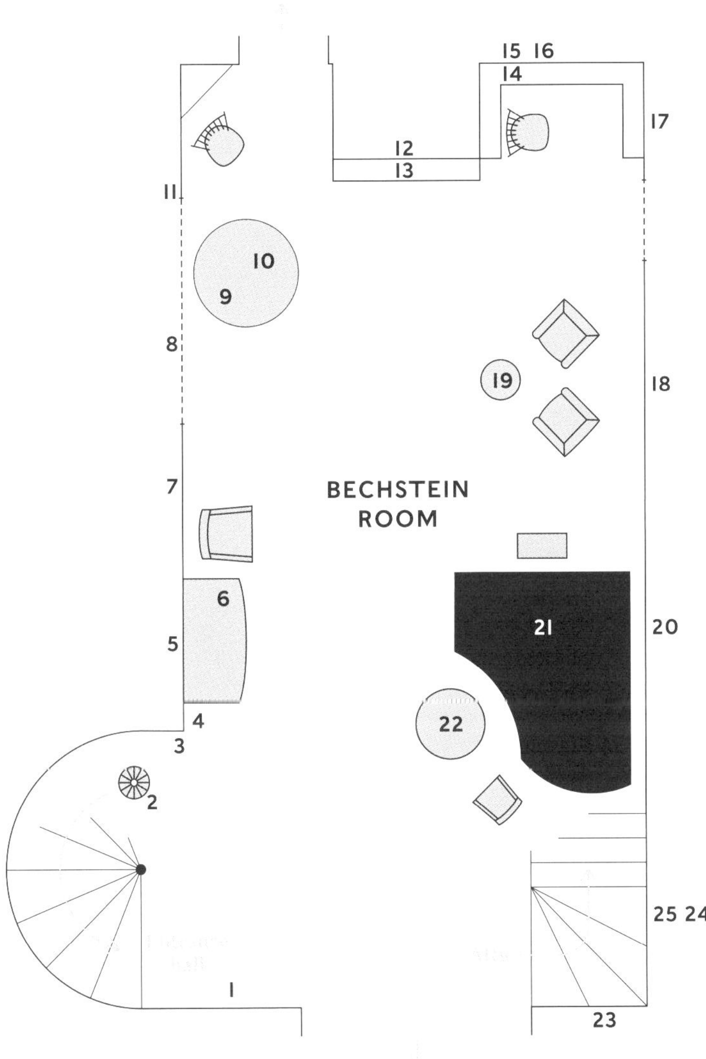
BECHSTEIN
ROOM
1
2
3
4
5
6
7
8
9
10
11
12
13
14
15 16
17
18
19
20
21
22
23
25 24

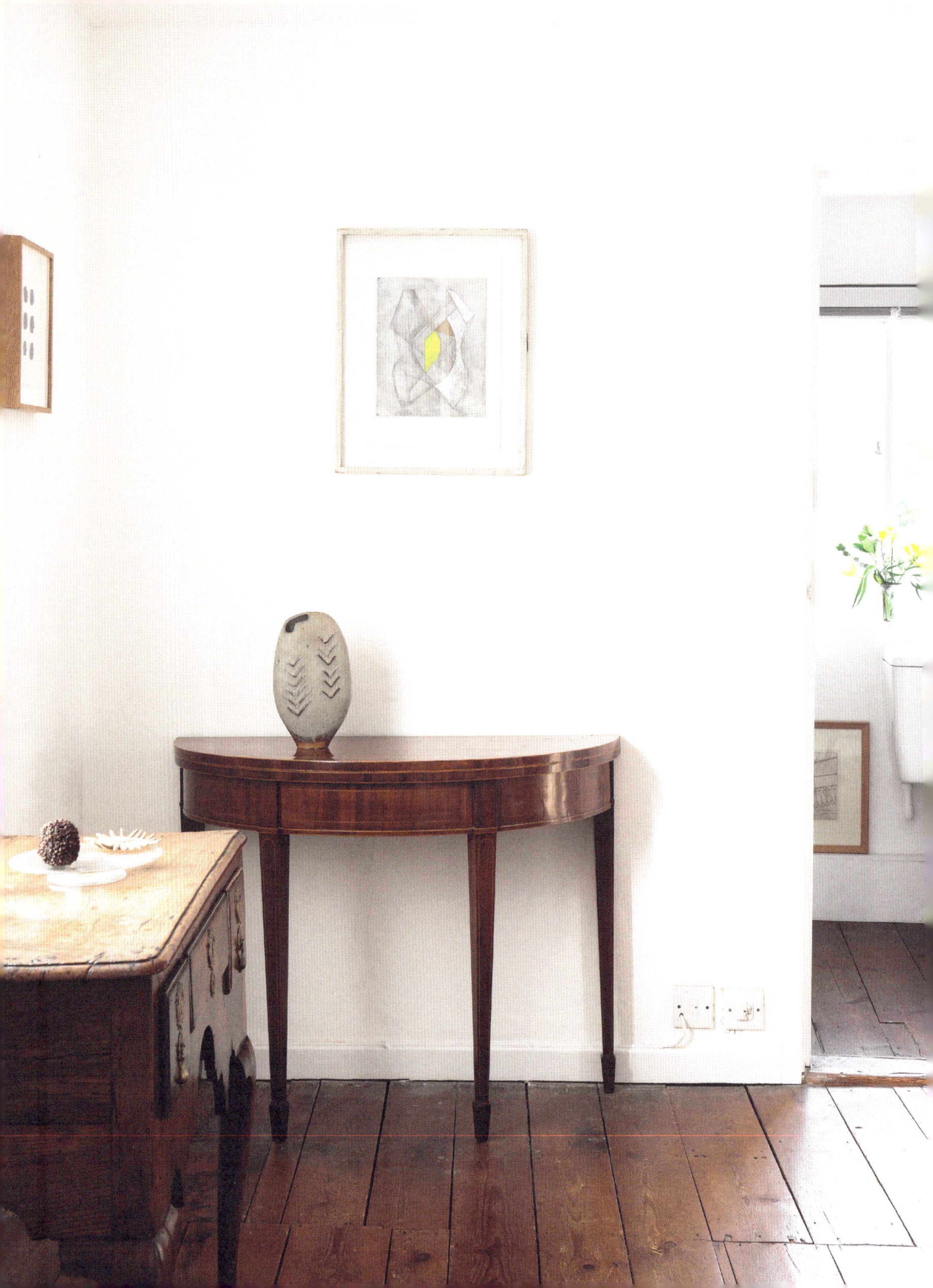

HELEN EDE'S BEDROOM AND BATHROOM

While the Edes were living at Kettle's Yard, Helen Ede's bedroom and bathroom remained a private space that was not accessible to those visiting the house. Grandchildren Jane and Quince remember her room as an informal space, in contrast to the spaces elsewhere in the house. Jane recalls 'sewing, everywhere', and children's drawings, which their grandmother always showed an interest in. Quince remembers more functional items – the ironing board and her grandmother's sewing machine, as well as many books. After the Edes left the house in 1973 and moved to Edinburgh, Helen Ede's bedroom was used as an office for the staff who cared for the house and ran the gallery. This is something Jim Ede later complained about, writing in 1977 to restate his hope that it may 'become a very beautiful extension to the sitting room'. Not long afterwards, the bedroom was reintegrated into the publicly accessible parts of the house and used as a space to hang artworks from the collection in storage. Over the years, it has also been used for contemporary artists' projects. One such intervention remains in this room – on the window that overlooks the churchyard are marks made in Dover chalk by artist Cornelia Parker for an exhibition at Kettle's Yard in 2018.

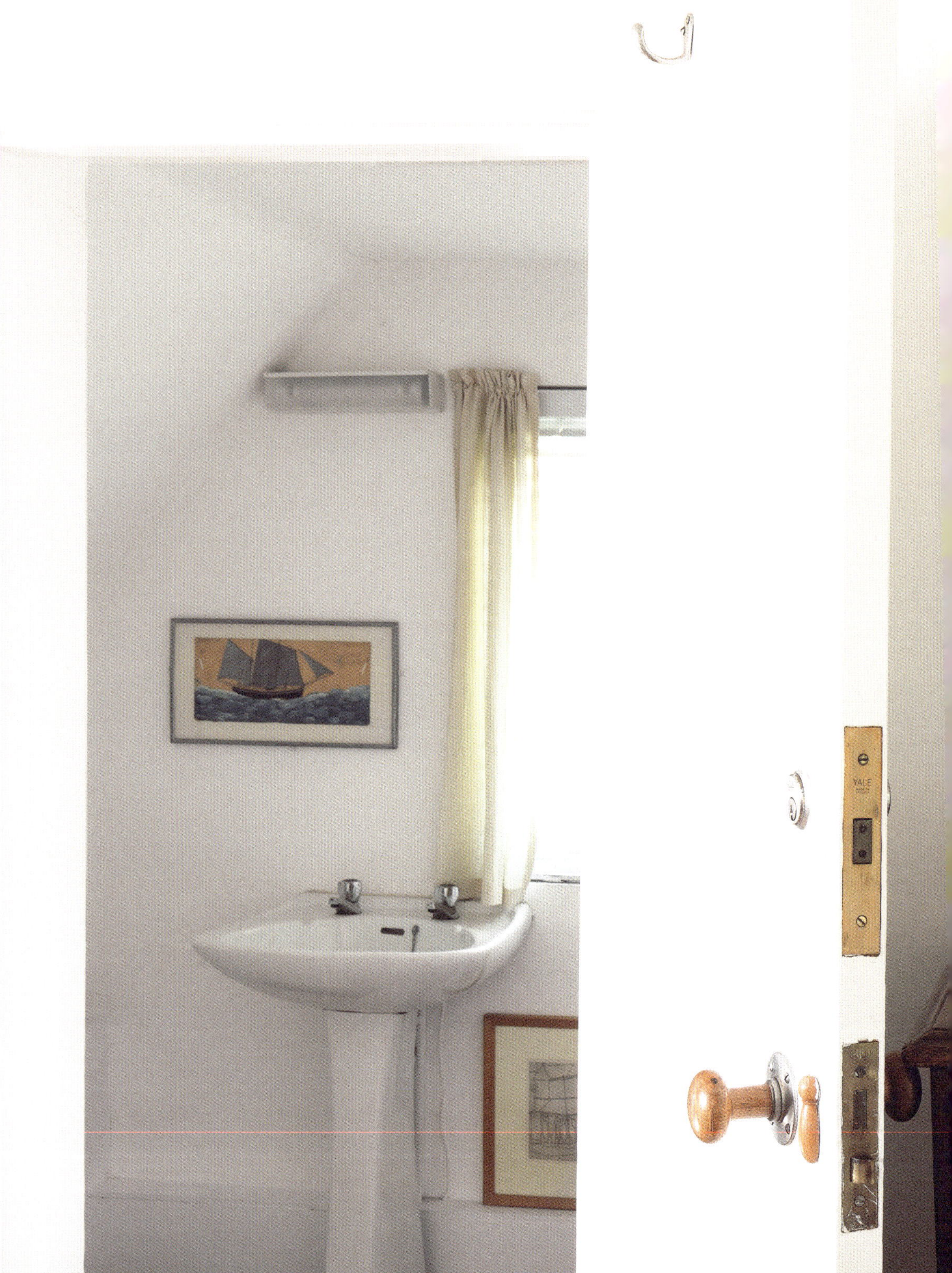
YALE

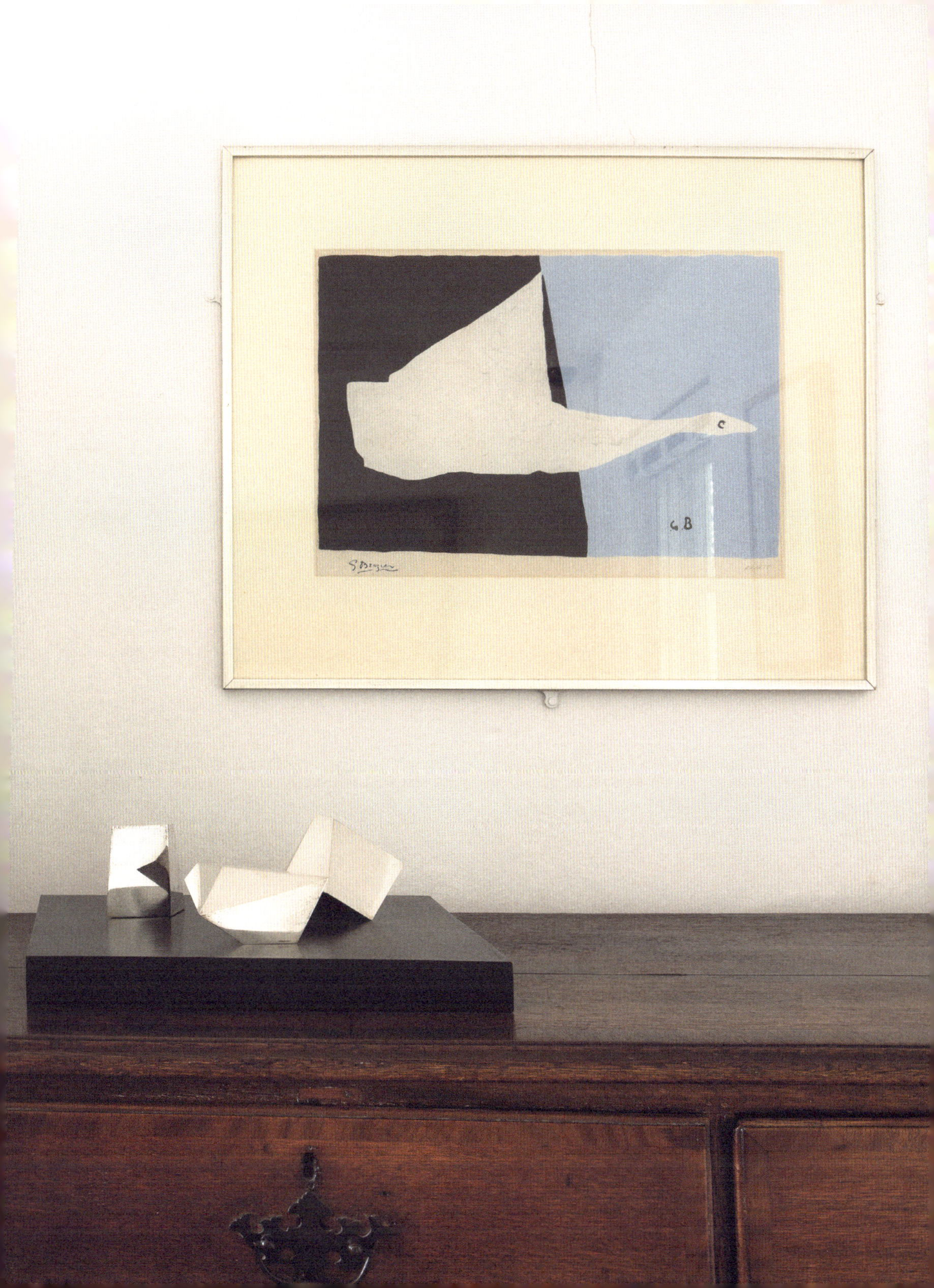

BEDROOM

1 Richard Pousette-Dart
Group of rings, c. 1940–50
Brass and jade
KY00759.EH

2 Naum Gabo
Negative Volume, 1940
Oil paint on coco de mer
KY01357

3 Ben Nicholson
1943 (abstract paper relief), 1943
Gouache and graphite on card
KY00755.E

4 Ben Nicholson
Abstract Box, 1933
Oil paint and graphite on strawboard box
KY00701.EH

5 Ben Nicholson
1934 (first scheme for massine ballet), 1934
Etching on paper
KY00642.E

6 Naum Gabo
Alabaster Carving (aka The Bobbin), 1938
Alabaster
KY01351

7 Naum Gabo
Round Stone, undated
Stone
KY01353

8 Naum Gabo
Miniature Carving, c. 1960–70
White stone
KY01352

9 Naum Gabo
Amulet, undated
Pink stone
KY01359

10 Winifred Nicholson
White Saxifrage (aka Wild Lilies, Greece), 1966
Watercolour on paper
KY00925.E

11 Cornelia Parker
Untitled, 2018
Chalk on window glazing
KY01440

12 Abani Roy
Indian Scene, undated
Pen and ink on paper
KY00386.E

13 Chest of drawers, England, 18th century
Wood and metal
KY00027

14 Georges Braque
Le Cygne volant, late 1950s
Lithograph on paper
KY00768.E

15 Barbara Hepworth
Group of Three Magic Stones, 1973
Silver on black lacquered wood base
KY01253

16 Barbara Hepworth
Group for sculpture (contrapuntal forms), 1947
Oil paint and graphite on card mounted on hardboard
KY01251

or William Scott
Message Obscure I, 1956
Oil paint on canvas
KY00928.EH

17 Zoë Ellison
Grey Flattened Vase, c. 1959
Glazed stoneware
KY01206

18 Sophie Taeuber-Arp
Dessin, 1915
Graphite on paper
KY01376

or Vicken Parsons
Buttons, 2023
Stoneware glazed with ultramarine slip

19 Starfish, undated
KY00374.E

20 Pomander, 20th century
Orange and cloves
KY00375.E

21 Issam Kourbaj
Urgent archives, written in blood (fragment), 2019
Ink on paper
KY01435

BATHROOM

22 David Jones
Tailpiece for 'The Rime of the Ancient Mariner', 1928
Engraving on paper
KY00347.E

23 Alfred Wallis
Three-master against a white sky, undated
Oil paint and graphite on card
KY00436.E

24 Zoë Ellison
Bowl (filled with pebbles), c. 1950s
Earthenware
KY01202

25 Ben Nicholson
Brissago, 1965
Etching on paper
KY01256.E

26 Alfred Wallis
French Lugsail fishing boat, undated
Oil paint on card
KY00445.E

27 Alan Reynolds
Study for 'Summer: Young September's Cornfield', 1954
Watercolour and ink on paper
KY01385

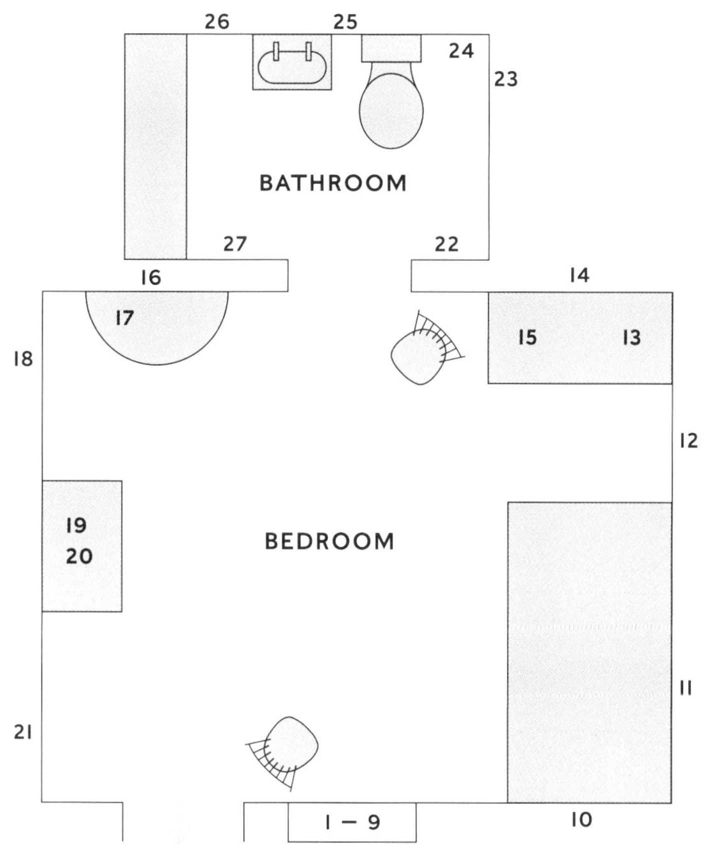
26
25
24
23
BATHROOM
27
22
16
14
17
15
13
18
12
19
20
BEDROOM
11
21
1 – 9
10

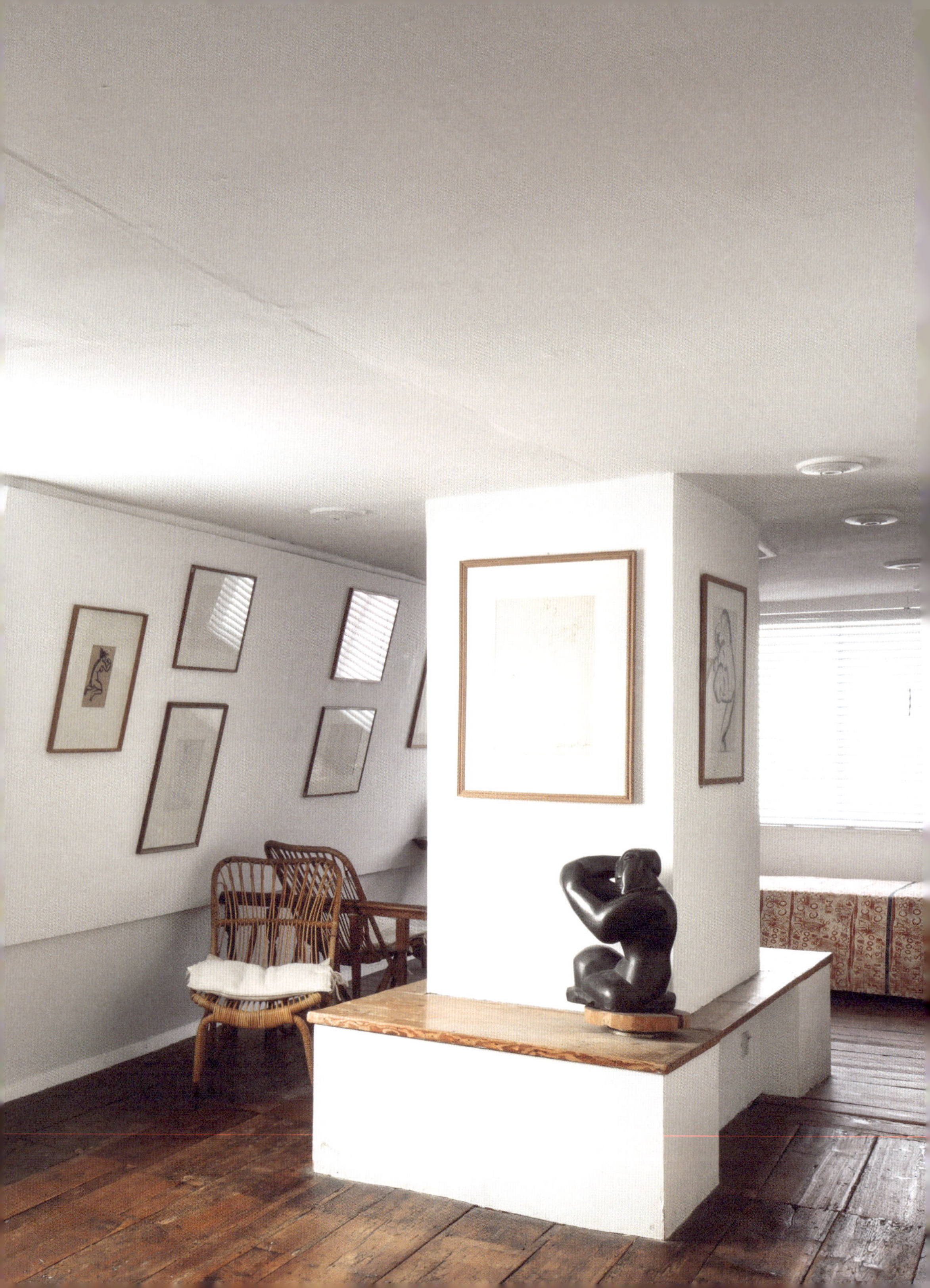

ATTIC

The low light levels in this space are maintained for conservation purposes and the works are frequently rotated to preserve their condition. A full list of works is available for visitors in the space.

Between 1957 and 1970, the attic rooms contained a mix of artworks, and it was here that the Edes' grandchildren slept when they came to stay. When the house was extended in 1970, many paintings and sculptures from the attic were transferred into the new areas. In their place, Jim Ede created a Henri Gaudier-Brzeska display, primarily of works on paper. To complement the Gaudier-Brzeskas, Jim Ede placed a sculpture by Ovidiu Maitec under one window. He was introduced to the Romanian-born artist's work in Edinburgh, by the gallerist Richard Demarco. Jim Ede was drawn to the mobile components of Maitec's sculpture and the way in which the holes in his carvings create patterns of light in a space. Other works introduced into this room more recently include a bedspread printed by Nancy Nicholson from a design by her brother Ben Nicholson. Above is a hanging mobile by the artist Li Yuan-chia, who was a friend of Winifred Nicholson and the subject of an exhibition in the gallery at Kettle's Yard in 2023–24.

1 Henri Gaudier-Brzeska, *Self-portrait with a pipe*, 1913
Graphite on paper
KY00566.EH

2 Henri Gaudier-Brzeska, *Self-portrait with a pipe*, 1913
Ink on paper
KY00567.EH

3 Henri Gaudier-Brzeska, *Self-portrait with a pipe*, 1913
Charcoal on paper
KY00568.EH

4 Spider conch shell, undated
KY00148

5 Henri Gaudier-Brzeska
Samson and Delilah (The Embracers), 1913
Cast plaster
KY00372.EH

6 Ovidiu Maitec
Bird, c. 1969
Walnut wood
KY01137.EH

7 Henri Gaudier-Brzeska
Seated Woman, 1914 (cast 1964)
Bronze
KY01152.EH

8 Skull-shaped stone from Henri Gaudier-Brzeska's studio, undated
KY01150.EH

9 Li Yuan-chia
Untitled, 1968
Paint on metal, MDF, mirror, nails
KY01433

10 Ben Nicholson printed by Nancy Nicholson (1899-1977)
letters and numbers, c. 1933
Lino block print on cotton
KY01430

11 Henri Gaudier-Brzeska
Maternity (Mother and Child), 1913 (cast 1960s)
Bronze
KY00810.E

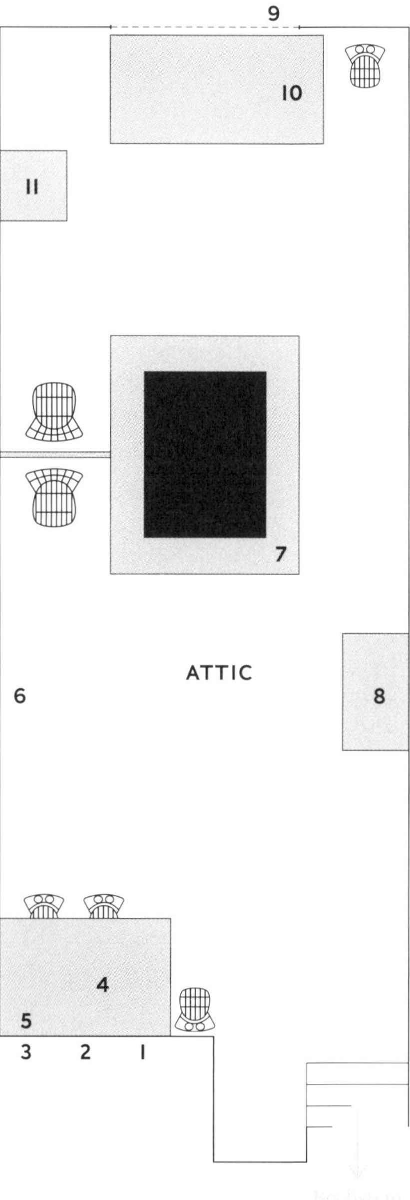

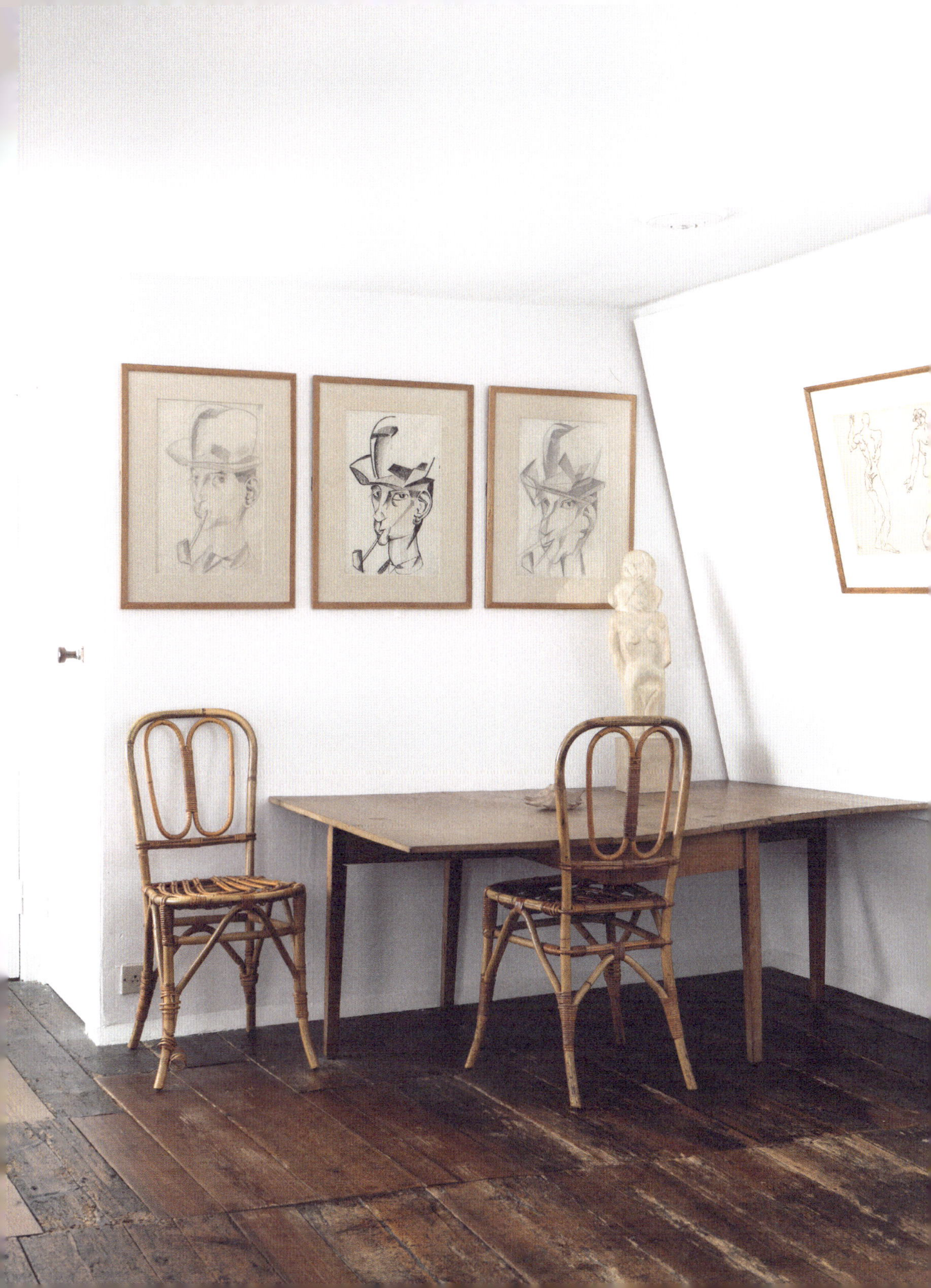

BRIDGE

The space known as the Bridge is situated directly over the alleyway entrance to the house, which is a public right of way. It joins the three-storey nineteenth-century cottages on one side to the two-story seventeenth-century cottage on the other. A small conservatory of plants, interspersed with artworks, shells, stones and other objects, emphasise the living, growing nature of the Kettle's Yard house and collection.

Jim Ede recalls finding the glass fisherman's floats (used to hold up nets) on the shores of the West Coast of the United States, 'like jewels in the early morning sunlight'. The shelves in front of the window hold several species of pelargonium, a 'pilea peperomioides' which originates in the Yunnan Province in China, a 'tradescantia zebrina' and a 'crassula ovata' or Jade plant. Many of the plants are grown from the cuttings of those from Jim and Helen Ede's time at Kettle's Yard. On the shelf above the steps down into the next space are blue and white Staffordshire ceramics, a painted nineteenth-century Coalport jug and three early nineteenth-century glass decanters made in Bohemia (now part of the Czech Republic).

1 Elisabeth Vellacott
Bare Trees and Hills, c. 1960
Graphite on paper
KY00803.EH

or *Trees*, c. 1970
Graphite on paper
KY01293

2 Gregorio Vardanega
Spherical Construction, c. 1963
Plexiglass
KY00895.EH

3 Breastbone of a bird, undated
KY00161.EH

4 Gregorio Vardanega
Disc, c. 1960
Plexiglass
KY00894.EH

5 William Staite Murray
Jar (The Heron), c. 1928
Glazed stoneware
KY00635.EH

6 Ben Nicholson
1944 (mugs), 1944
Oil paint and graphite on board
KY00756.EH

7 Henri Gaudier-Brzeska
Dog, 1914 (cast 1965)
Bronze
KY00869.EH

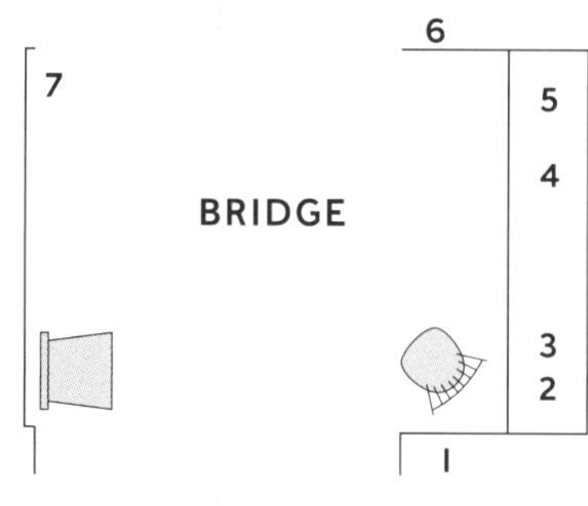

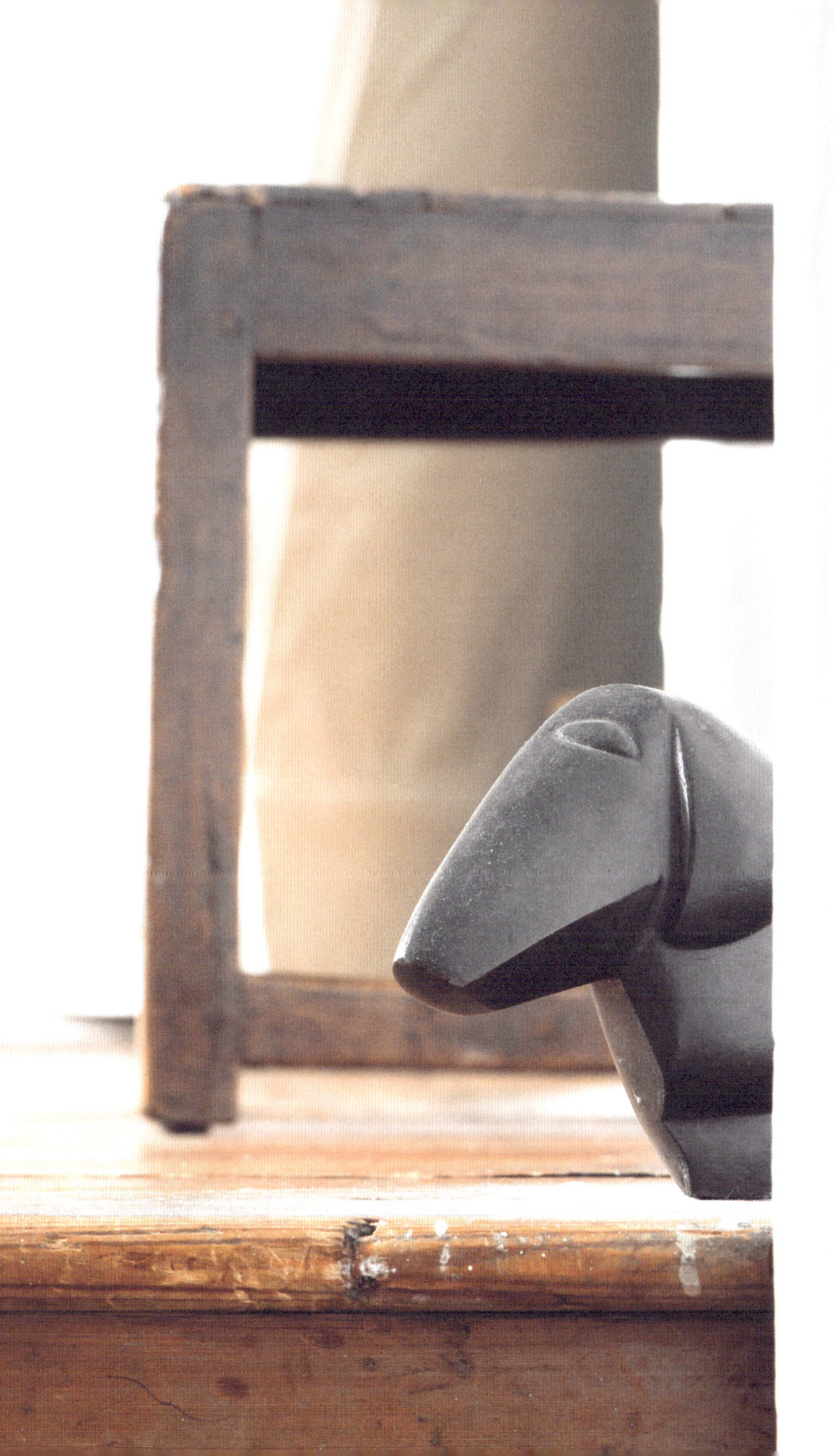

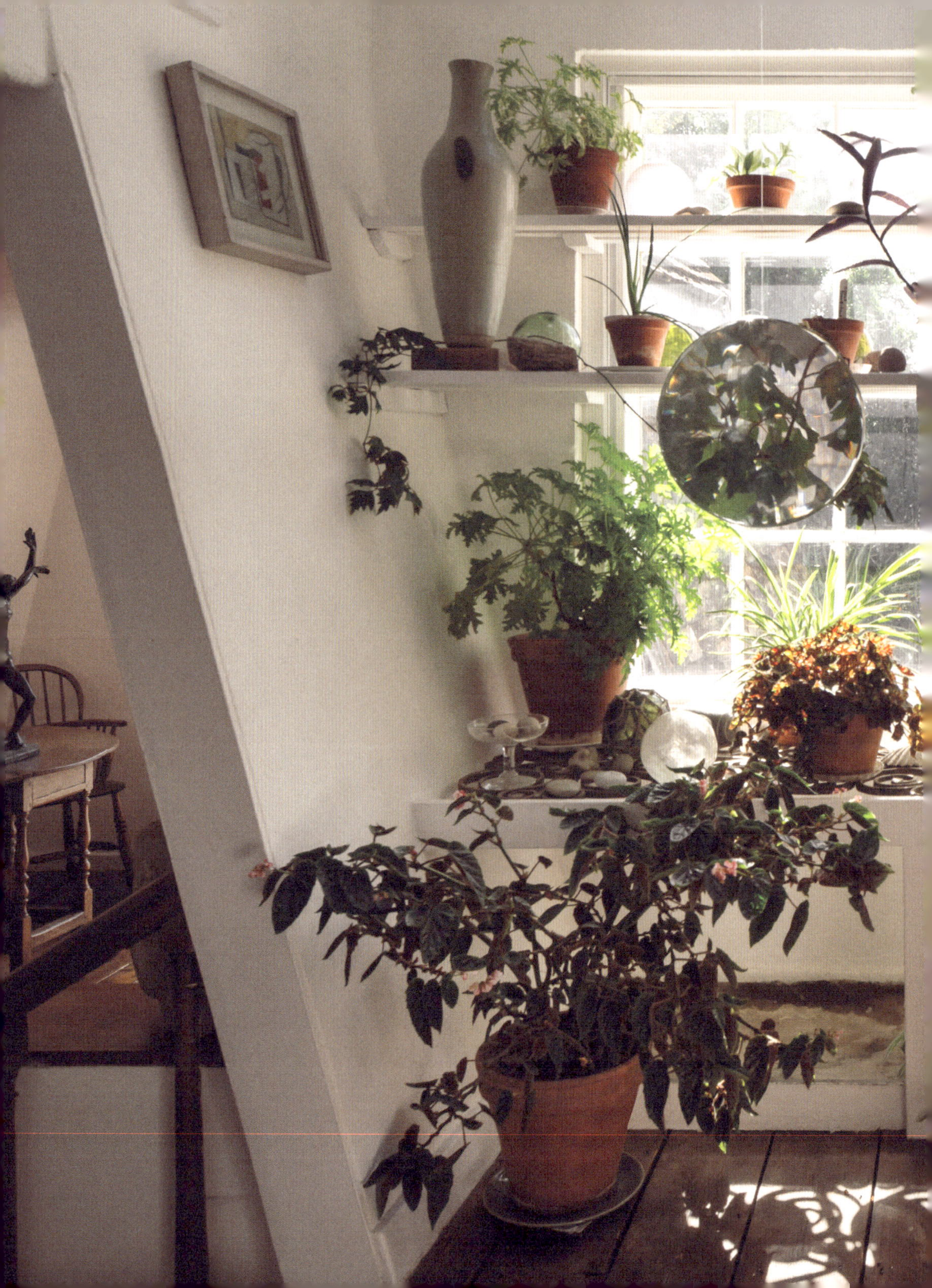

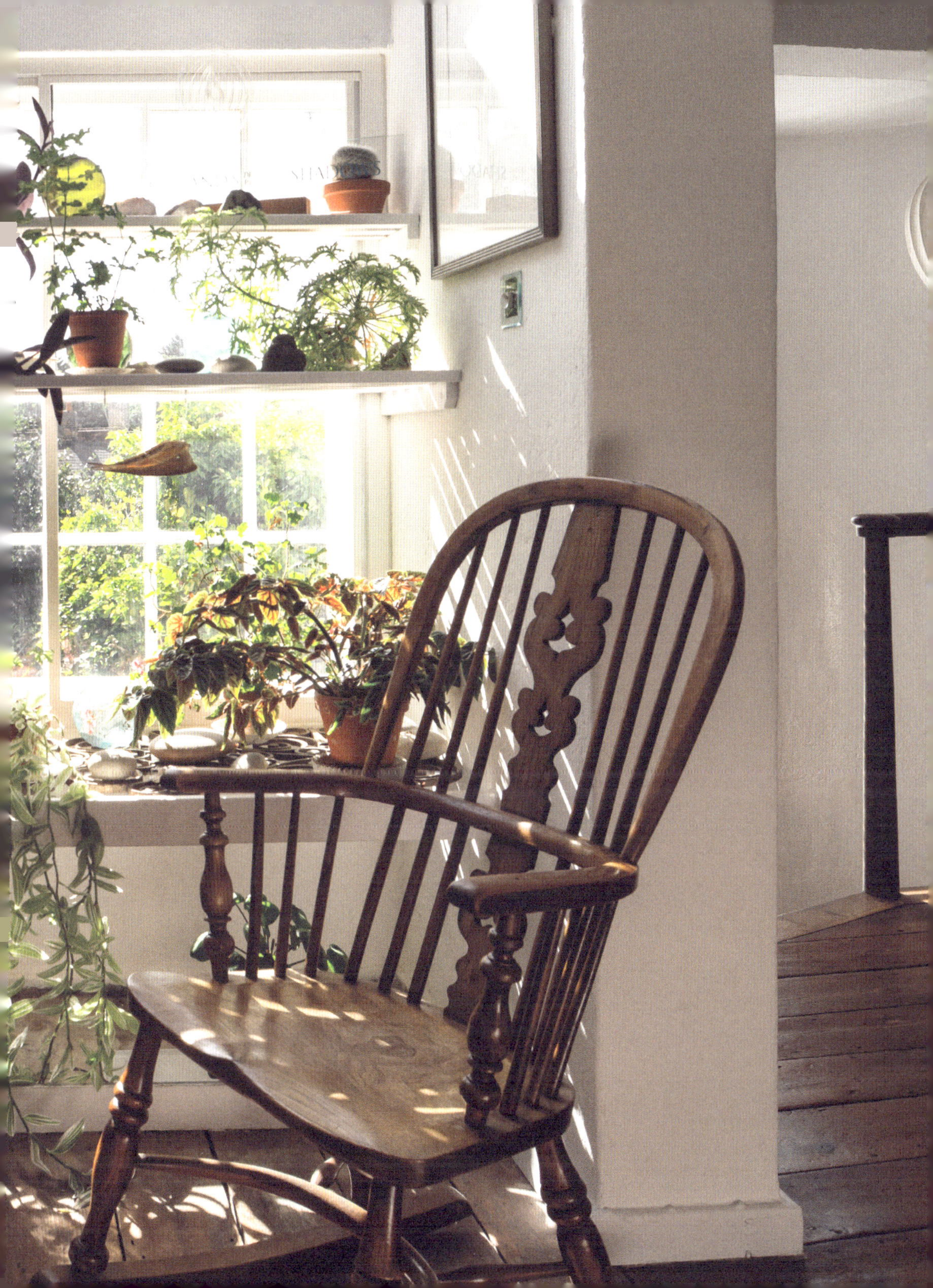

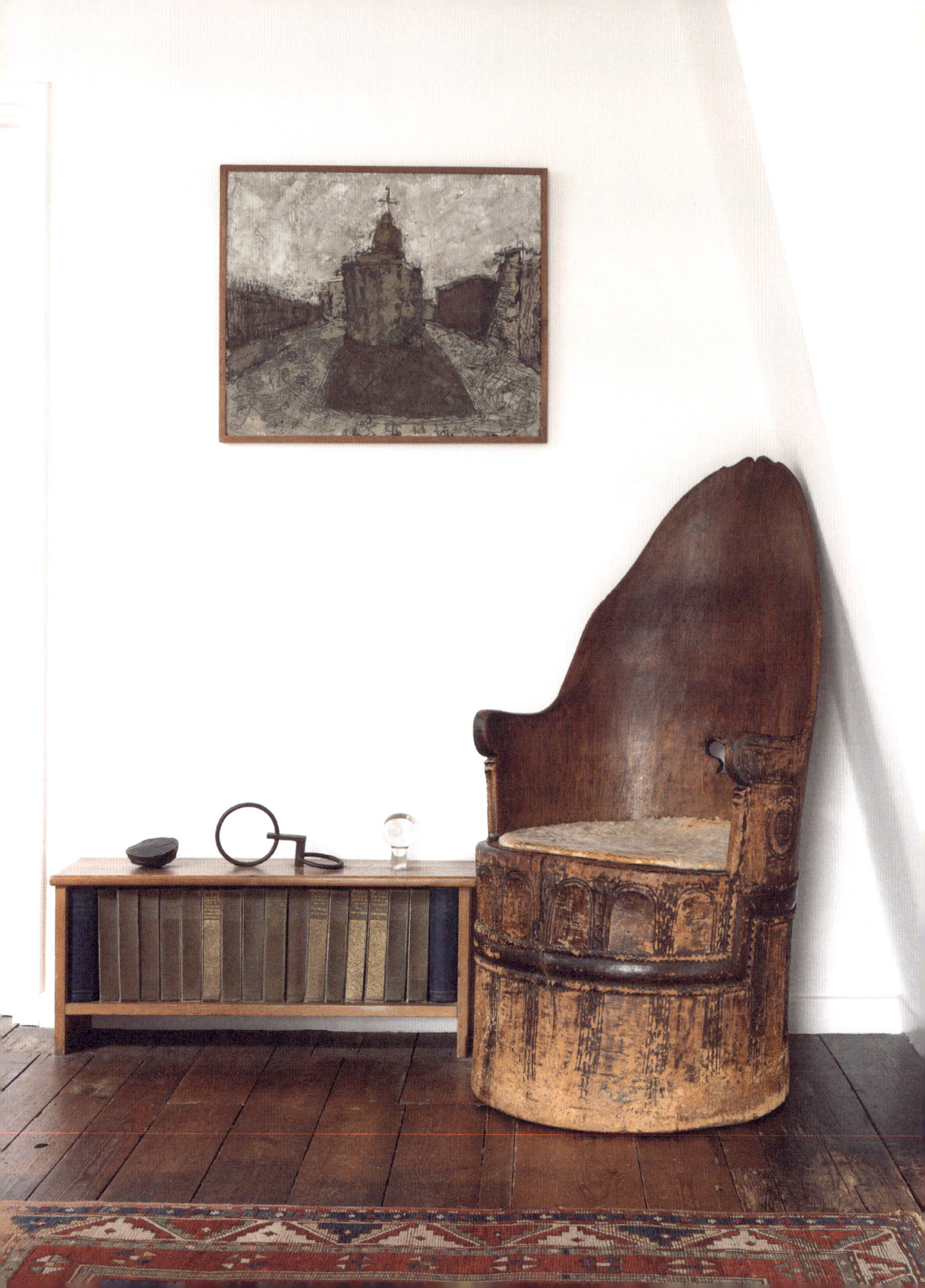

DANCER ROOM

This room is lit by a large southwest-facing early eighteenth-century window. It was salvaged from a grand house at 62 St. Andrew's Street in Cambridge. Known as Rance's Folly, the house was being demolished at the same time the Edes were refurbishing Kettle's Yard. The wrought iron plant shelves on the Bridge, as well as the wood for the spiral staircase, were also salvaged from the same house. The rugs in this space are from Iran and the South-West Caucasus region. The influence of the Romanian-born artist Constantin Brâncuși can be observed in this room: the Norwegian 'kubbestol' chair, carved from a single piece of wood, is reminiscent of some of Brâncuşi's folk-style carvings, and the carved paperknife on the bookshelves is remarkably similar to Brâncuşi's sculpture *Hand of Mademoiselle Pogany* (1920) in the collection of Harvard Art Museums. Jim Ede often visited the sculptor's studio in Paris while he was working at the Tate Gallery. There, Brâncuși's hand-carved furniture sat alongside polished metal sculptures, against white-washed walls lit from the glass roof above, and flowers that 'seemed never to wilt'. Brâncuşi died in 1957 and left his studio and its contents to the French state, something Jim Ede had earlier advised upon.

1 Ben Nicholson
1958 (jugs 'criss cross'), 1958
Graphite and watercolour on card
KY00788.EH

2 John Blackburn
Lead relief, c. 1963
Lead and oil paint mounted on wood
KY00859.EH

3 Michael Pine
Construction, 1955
Plaster
KY00824.EH

4 Elisabeth Vellacott
Portrait of Gwen Raverat, 1954
Pencil on paper
KY00892.EH

5 Tam MacPhail
Construction, c. 1968
Iron
KY00937.EH

6 William Congdon
Naples-Church, 1950
Oil paint on hardboard
KY00775.EH

7 'Kubbestol' chair and cushion, Norway, undated
Pine wood, straw and hide
KY000340.EH

8 Max Ernst
Figure, 1925
Graphite on paper
KY00927.EH

9 Christopher Wood
Landscape with Figures, c. 1926
Oil paint on canvas
KY00341.EH

10 Henri Gaudier-Brzeska
Dancer, 1913 (cast 1967)
Bronze
KY00818.EH

11 George Kennethson
Construction (Birds), c. 1968
Staffordshire alabaster
KY00917.EH

12 William Congdon
Piazza San Marco no.25, 1957
Oil paint on hardboard
KY00774.EH

13 William Congdon
Luna 7, Subiaco, 1967
Oil paint on hardboard
KY00830.EH

14 Painted and lacquered tray, 18th century
Papier-mâché, paint, varnish
KY00038.EH

15 Simon Kenrick
Design (Stonehenge), undated
Collage and oil paint on board
KY00828.EH

16 Flat-woven striped cloth, Morocco, 20th century
KY01101.EH

17 Henri Gaudier-Brzeska
Head, 1913 (cast 1964)
Cast stone
KY00812.EH

18 Carved paperknife, undated
Wood
KY00237.EH

19 Henri Gaudier-Brzeska
Mermaid, 1912-13
Marble
KY00488.EH

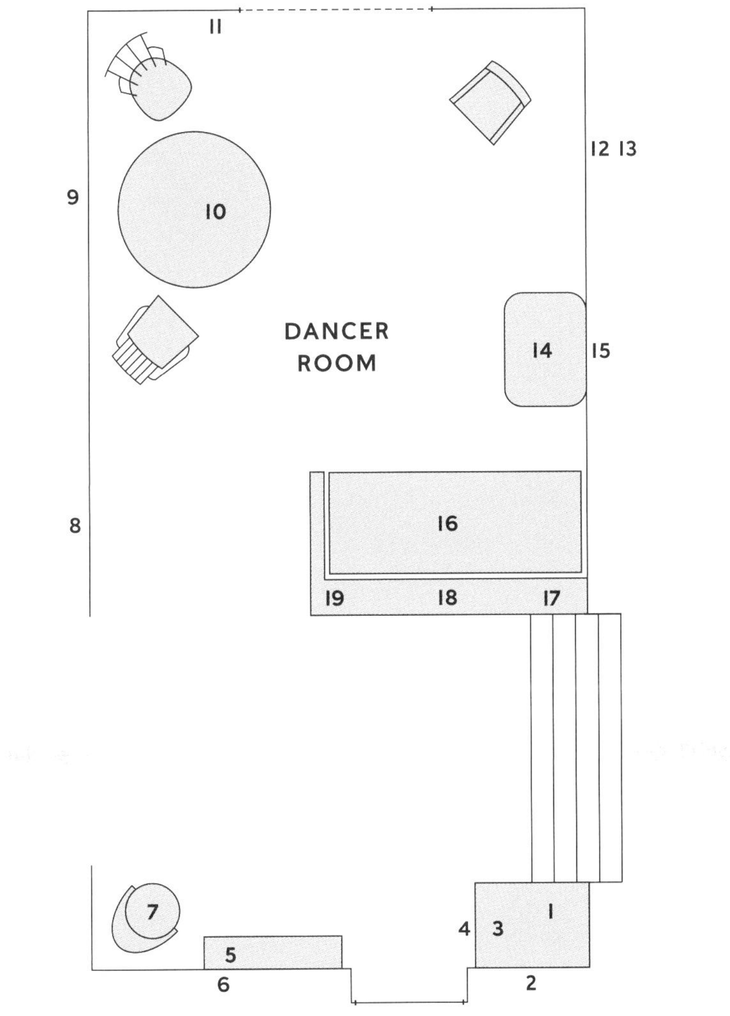
11
12 13
9
10
DANCER
ROOM
14
15
8
16
19
18
17
7
1
4
3
5
6
2

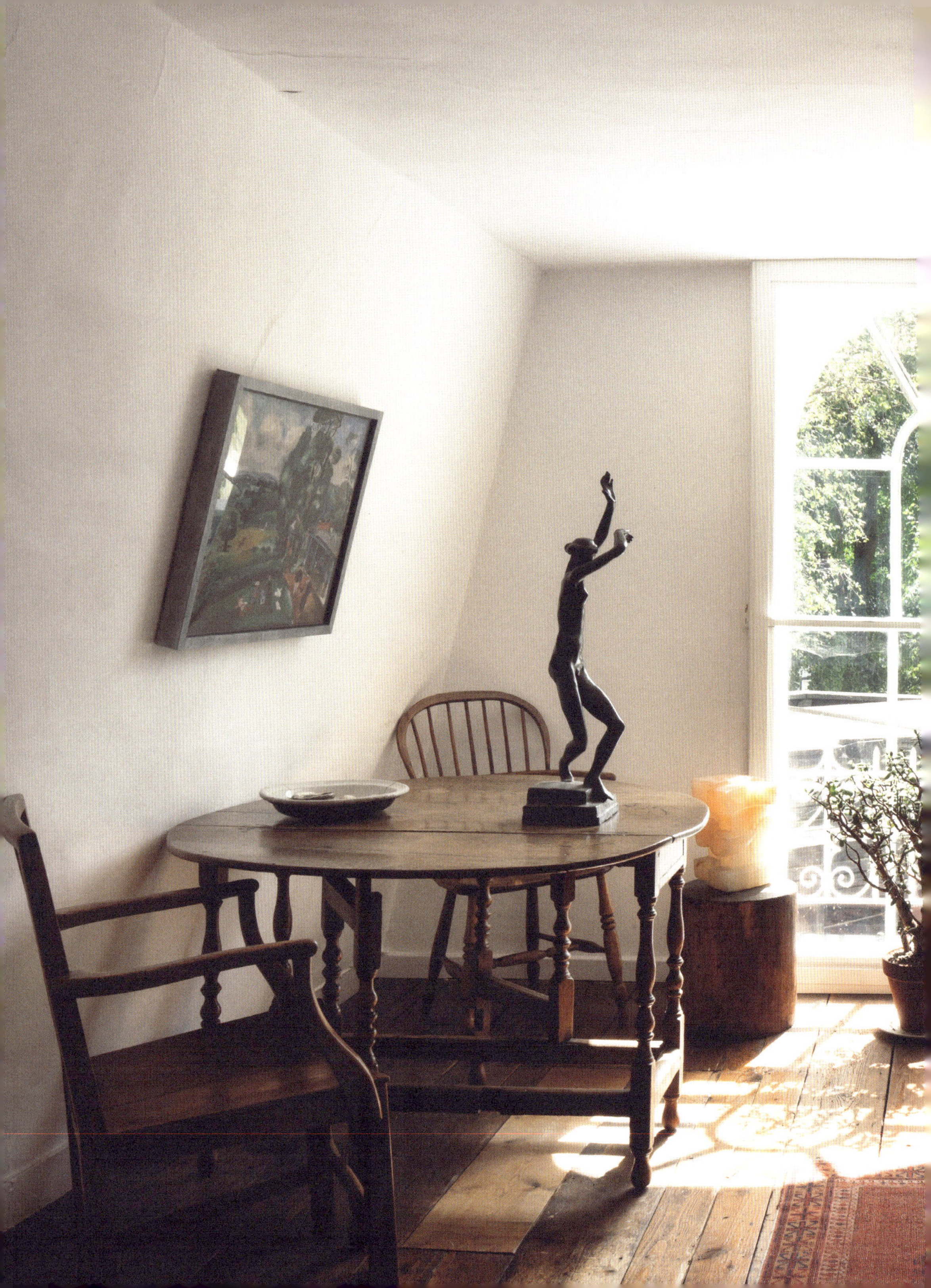

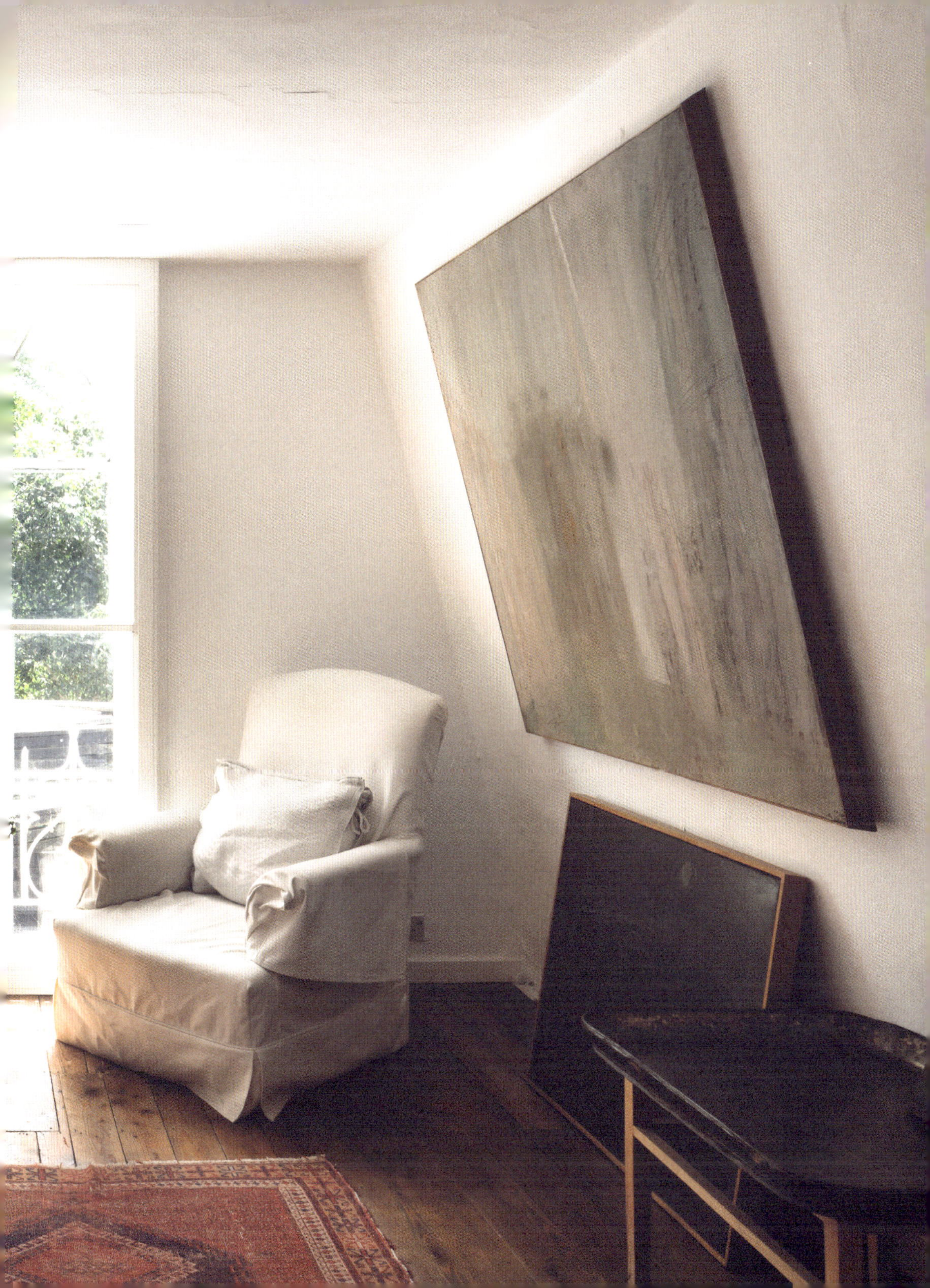

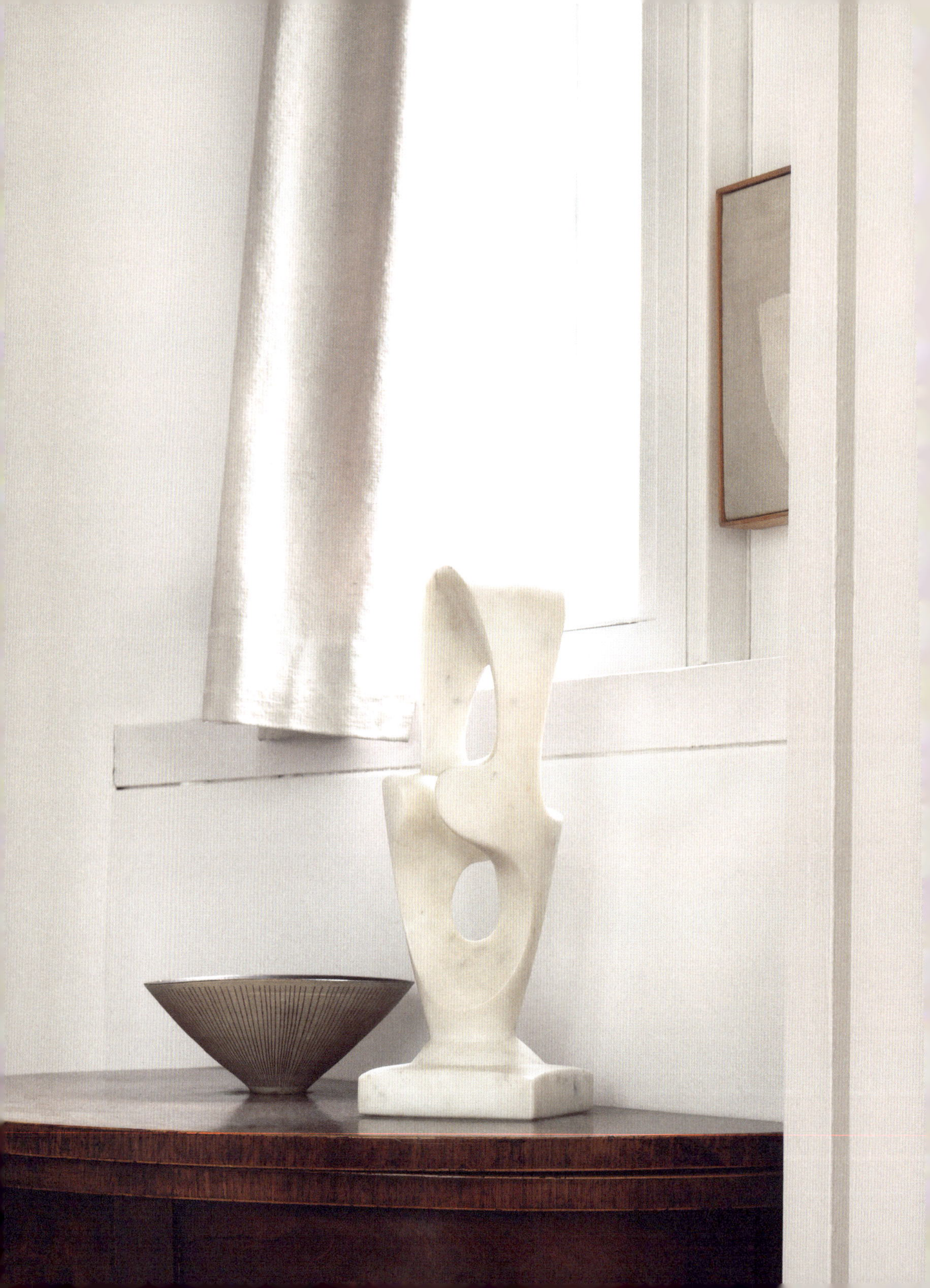

LINK

Down the steps via works by Lucie Rie, Kenji Umeda, William Scott and Ben Nicholson, a small doorway leads from the irregular spaces of the cottages to the more linear spaces of the extension, completed and furnished in 1970. The Edes' friend Sir Leslie Martin was appointed as the architect, designing, in his words, a 'series of descending levels and top lit spaces'. Martin worked with fellow architect David Owers on the final designs, and Jim Ede maintained close involvement as the plans developed, writing to Owers frequently throughout the process. Owers described the materials of the cottages as 'various unpolished timbers, brick, rough plaster and slate, the colours: cool whites, faded blue, oatmeal, the natural hues of stone, shell, glass, tile, pewter and scrubbed wood'. This informed choices for the new building, which features 'rough plaster, second-hand brick paviors, natural pine'. The aim was to retain 'the ambience of a home', even though 'the function of the home' - with the space increased fourfold - 'would inevitably be modified'. Softening the architectural transition are various echoes of features in the cottages. A window of plants mirrors that on the Bridge, today holding similar species as well as a 'Tiger Paws' begonia and a bromeliad plant, originating from Brazil. The wooden chest just to the right of the plants conceals a record player, which the adjacent seating faced for the purposes of listening.

1 Ben Nicholson
1928–9 (two mugs),
1928–29
Linocut print
on paper
KY00625.EH

2 Ben Nicholson
letters and numbers,
c. 1933
Linoblock print
on cotton
KY00705.EH

3 Lucie Rie
Bowl, c. 1960
Glazed porcelain
KY01104.EH

4 Kenji Umeda
Spirality, 1977
Marble
KY01111.EH

5 William Scott
Bowl (White on Grey),
1962
Oil paint on canvas
KY00921.EH

6 Doorstop,
19th century
Glass
KY00177

7 Puppet, Java, undated
Painted wood,
fabric and string
KY01022.EH

8 Settee, England,
mid-18th century
Oak wood
KY01078.EH

9 William Congdon
Canal, Venice (Venice from the Giudecca),
1952
Oil paint on
hardboard
KY00770.EH

10 Armchair, Spain,
late 17th century
Walnut wood
KY00485.EH

11 William Congdon
The Black City I (New York), 1949
Oil paint, enamel
paint and ink on
hardboard
KY00898.EH

12 Lantern, Japan,
19th century
Cloth and wood
R00052

13 David Peace
Canst thou bind the cluster of the pleiades or loose the bands of orion, 1961
Engraved glass
KY01138.EH

14 Ben Nicholson
1965 (goblet), 1965
Pen, ink and
wash on paper
KY00899.EH

15 Alberto Burri
Buon, c. 1960
Paint and paper
on board
KY01365

16 Chest, France,
19th century
Walnut wood
KY00047.EH

17 William Congdon
India Temples no. 1 (Sri Ranganathaswamy Temple, Tiruchirappalli), 1954
Oil paint, gold paint
and enamel paint on
hardboard
KY00785.EH

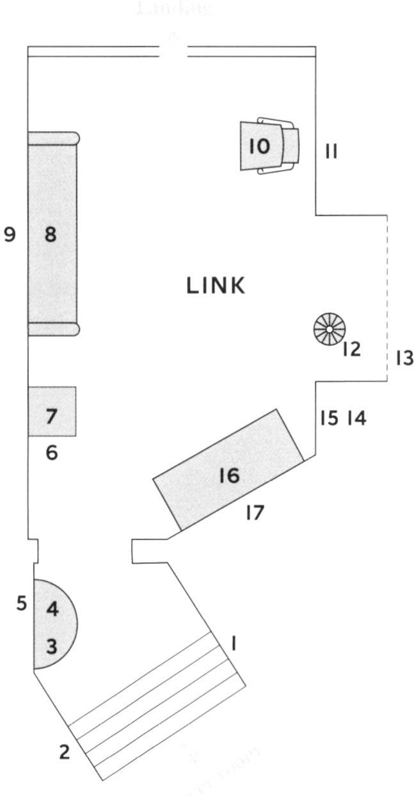

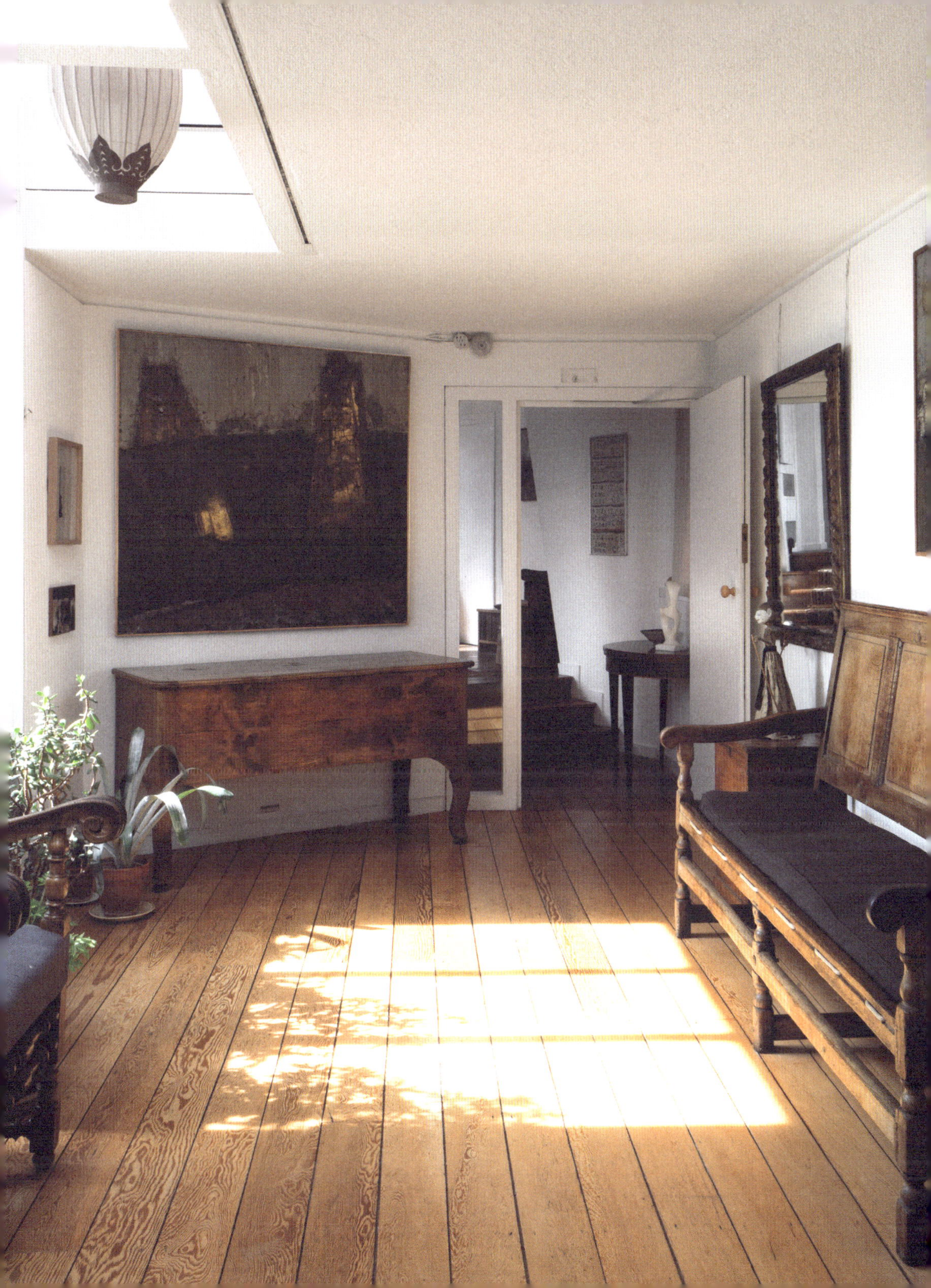

LANDING

The large oval table was previously used as the Edes' dining table at Elm Row in Hampstead, and travelled with them to Morocco and France, before finally being placed here at Kettle's Yard. The large stone upon it was known as the 'Brâncuși stone', comparable in size and shape to Brâncuși's 1920 sculpture *The Beginning of the World*, now in the collection of the Dallas Museum of Art. Barbara Hepworth's sculpture *Three Personages* was purchased by Jim Ede after he visited the artist's 1968 retrospective exhibition at the Tate Gallery. Ede wrote to Hepworth to enquire about the work, which she explained was 'really part of my private collection', but promised, 'for you I would do all I could'.

1 Zartoshti-duzi (Zoroastrian embroidery) trouser textile, Iran, late 19th or early 20th century
Embroidered cotton
KY01147.EH

2 Ben Nicholson
1930 (Christmas night), 1930
Oil paint and graphite on canvas
KY01131.EH

3 Henri Gaudier-Brzeska
Madonna (Maria Carmi as the Madonna), 1912
Painted plaster
KY00983.EH

4 Ben Nicholson
May 1927 (still life with knife and lemon), 1927
Oil paint on canvas
KY00333.EH

5 Bryan Pearce
King's College Chapel, 1966
Oil paint on hardboard
KY00914.EH

6 Ovidiu Maitec
Radar II, 1970
Walnut wood
KY01135.EH

7 Barbara Hepworth
Three Personages, 1965
Black slate on a wooden base
KY00979.EH

8 David Peace
'While thus they sing…', c. 1971
Engraved glass
KY01139.EH

9 Three-legged stool, France, 20th century
Wood
KY00778.EH

10 David Peace
Sanctuary lamp, 1955 (remade 1994)
Engraved glass
KY01000B.EH

11 Simon Nicholson
St Ives 12, 1962
Matches on strawboard
KY00940.EH

12 Alfred Wallis
White houses - Hales Down, near St Ives, 1930-32
Oil paint and graphite on card
KY00784.EH

13 Winifred Nicholson
Seascape with Dinghy, c. 1932
Oil paint on canvas
KY01261.EH

14 'Brâncuși stone', undated
KY00197.EH

15 Henri Gaudier-Brzeska
Caritas, 1914 (posthumous cast)
Cast stone
KY00819.EH

16 Elisabeth Vellacott
Entangled Trees, 1976
Graphite on paper
KY01107.EH

17 Winifred Nicholson
Roman Road (Landscape with House and Barn), 1926
Oil paint on canvas
KY01260.EH

18 Elisabeth Vellacott
Trees and Water - Moat of the Manor, Hemingford Grey, 1971
Graphite on paper
KY01132.EH

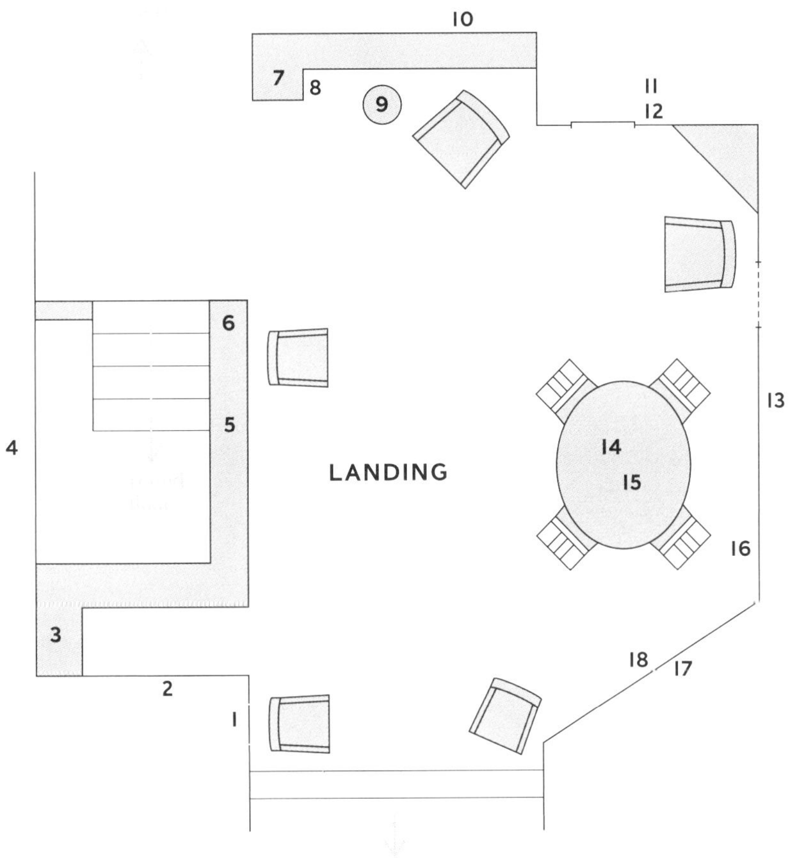
10
7
8
9
11
12
6
5
4
LANDING
14
15
13
16
3
2
1
18
17

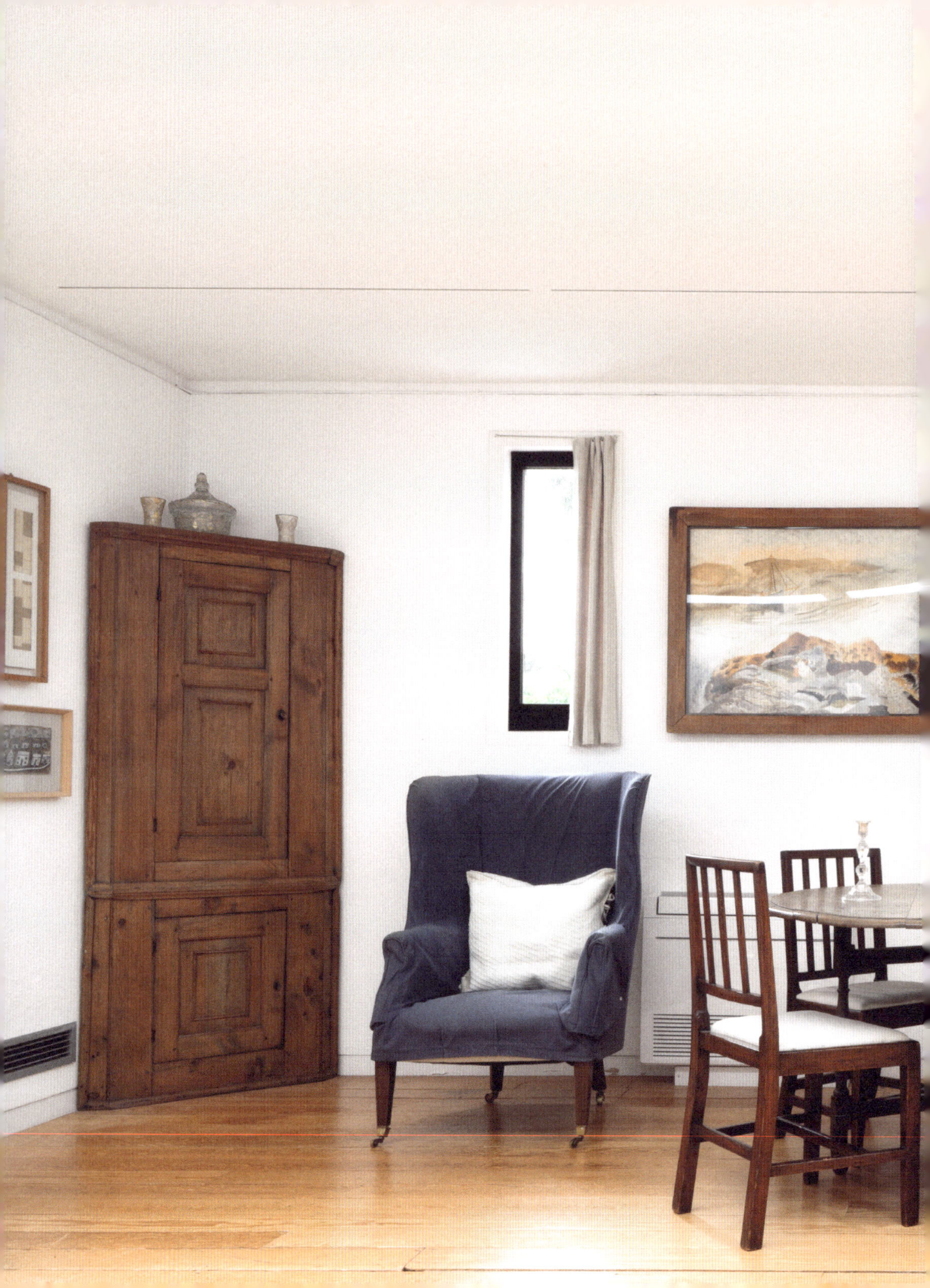

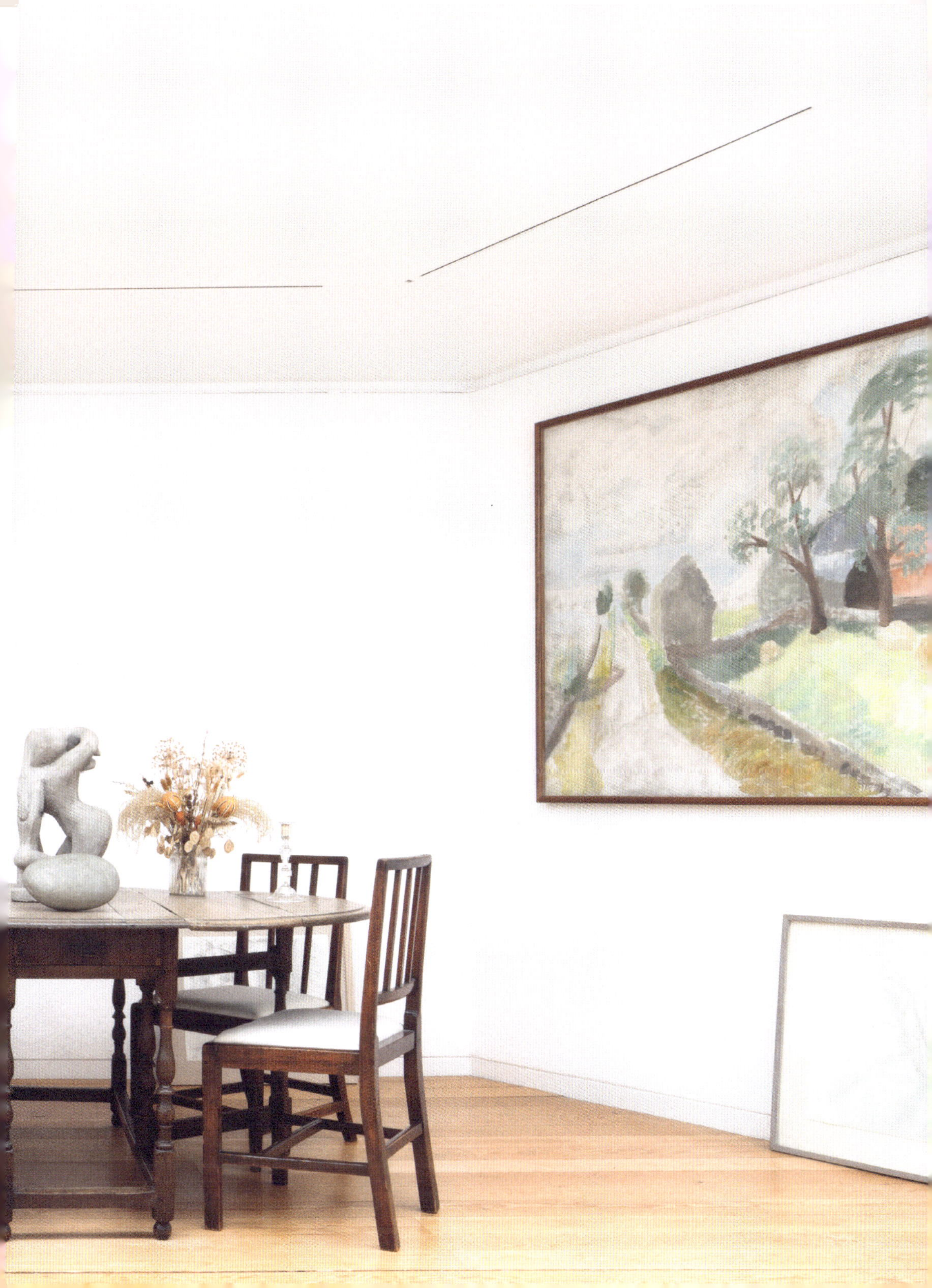

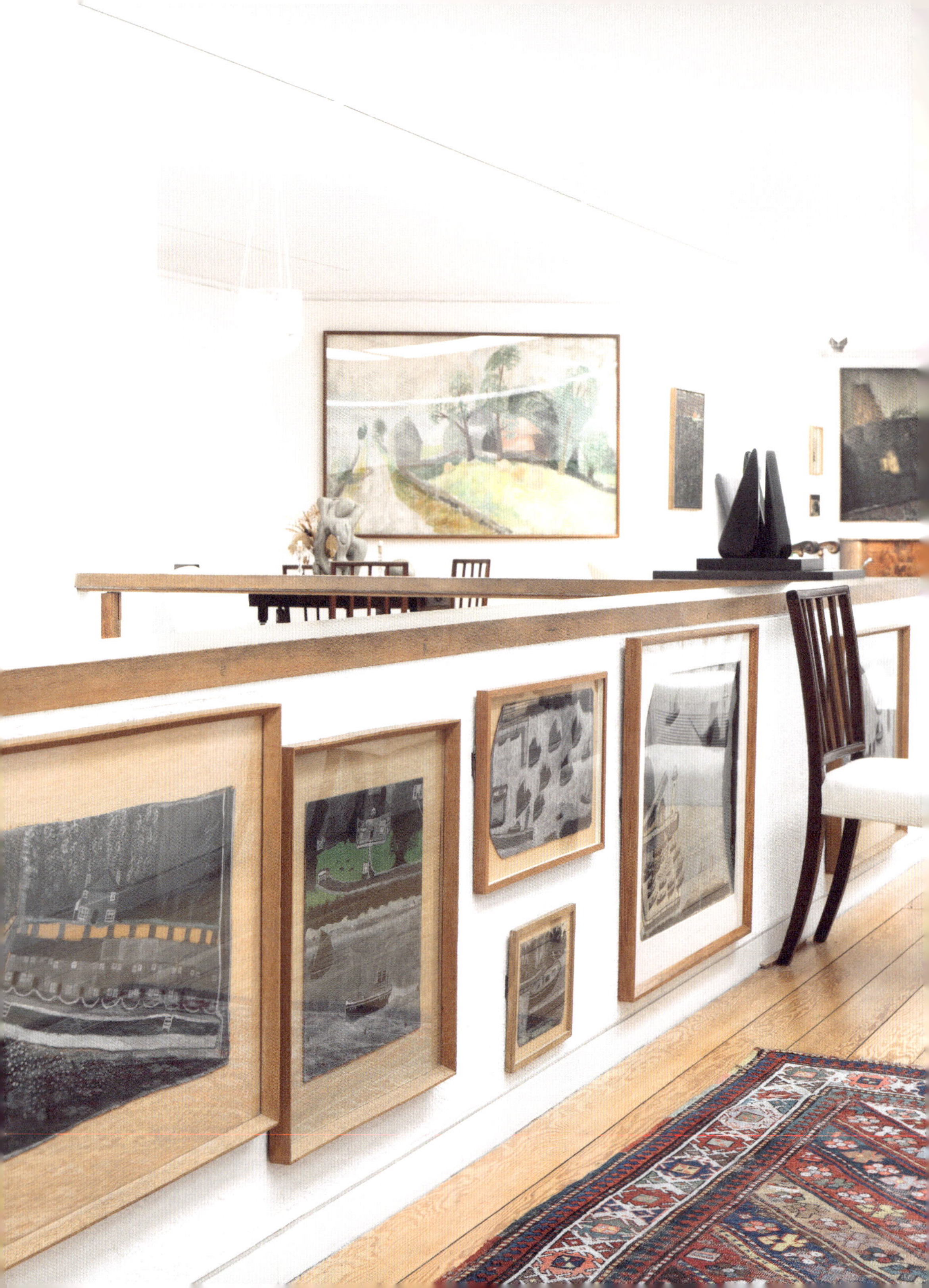

GALLERY

As the Martin-Owers extension neared completion in late December 1969, Jim Ede wrote in eager anticipation of the arrival of artworks into the space. 'I should start placing everything in a week or two - the ground floor is promised for the 31st but I can't believe it', he noted. He spent a few days 'living on the first floor' of the new building, after which, he wrote, 'I begin to see my way towards a unity'. As well as Windsor chairs and eighteenth-century armchairs, works by Ben and Winifred Nicholson, Christopher Wood and Henri Gaudier-Brzeska were moved across from the cottages to the extension. Jim Ede delighted in the increased wall space, which gave him an opportunity to present a large proportion of his substantial collection of paintings by Alfred Wallis, who Jim Ede never met but corresponded with frequently. Ede recieved parcels of Wallis's paintings in the post, priced by size, from which he would make a selection to purchase, and return the rest.

1 Bryan Pearce
The Round Church, Cambridge, c. 1966
Oil paint on hardboard
KY00913.EH

2 Tallboy, England, c. 1740-60
Oak and brass
KY00953.EH

3 Glassware, Beykoz, Turkey, late 19th century
Gilded glass
KY00840a-c.EH
KY00841a-c.EH
KY00845.EH

4 Alfred Wallis
Fishes and lobster pots, c.1936
Oil paint on card
KY00676.EH

5 Alfred Wallis
Flowering trees, undated
Oil paint on card
KY00417.EH

6 Alfred Wallis
Trees and cottages, c. 1935-37
Oil paint on card
KY00679.EH

7 Alfred Wallis
White house and cottages - the Old House, Porthmeor Square, 1930-32
Oil paint on card
KY00687.EH

8 Alfred Wallis
Shipwreck 2 - The Wreck of the Alba, 1938-40
Oil paint on card
KY00682.EH

9 Alfred Wallis
Boats before a great bridge (Royal Albert Bridge), c. 1935-37
Oil paint on card
KY00680.EH

10 Alfred Wallis
Portland, Dorset, undated
Oil paint on card
KY00420.EH

11 Alfred Wallis
Three-masted ship near lighthouse, 1928-30
Oil paint on board
KY00450.EH

12 Mirror frame, Florence, Italy, 18th century
Gilt and gesso paint on wood
KY00482.EH

13 Alfred Wallis
Penzance harbour, undated
Oil paint on card
KY00416.EH

14 Alfred Wallis
Two boats, undated
Oil paint on card
KY00428.EH

15 Alfred Wallis
P&O ship, undated
Oil paint on card
KY00421.EH

16 Alfred Wallis
Seven boats entering harbour, 1925-26
Oil paint on card
KY00403.EH

17 Alfred Wallis
Schooner in full sail near a lighthouse, c. 1925-28
Oil paint on card
KY00410.EH

18 Alfred Wallis
Boats under Saltash Bridge (Royal Albert Bridge), c. 1935-37
Oil paint on card
KY00677.EH

19 Henri Gaudier-Brzeska
Garden Ornament, 1914 (cast 1964)
Bronze
KY00872.EH

20 Alfred Wallis
Land, fish and motor vessel, c. 1932-37
Oil paint on card
KY00690.EH

21 Alfred Wallis
Street of houses and trees, undated
Oil paint on card
KY00433.EH

22 Alfred Wallis
Two boats moving past a big house, c. 1932-37
Oil paint on card
KY00688.EH

23 Alfred Wallis
Sailing ships and two steamers, Newlyn harbour, undated
Oil paint on board
KY00435.EH

24 Alfred Wallis
Ship, people and animals, undated
Oil paint on card
KY00429.EH

25 Alfred Wallis
Harbour with two lighthouses and motor vessel - St Ives Bay, c. 1932-34
Oil paint on card
KY00689.EH

26 Alfred Wallis
Mount's Bay with four lighthouses, undated
Oil paint, crayon and graphite on card
KY00409.EH

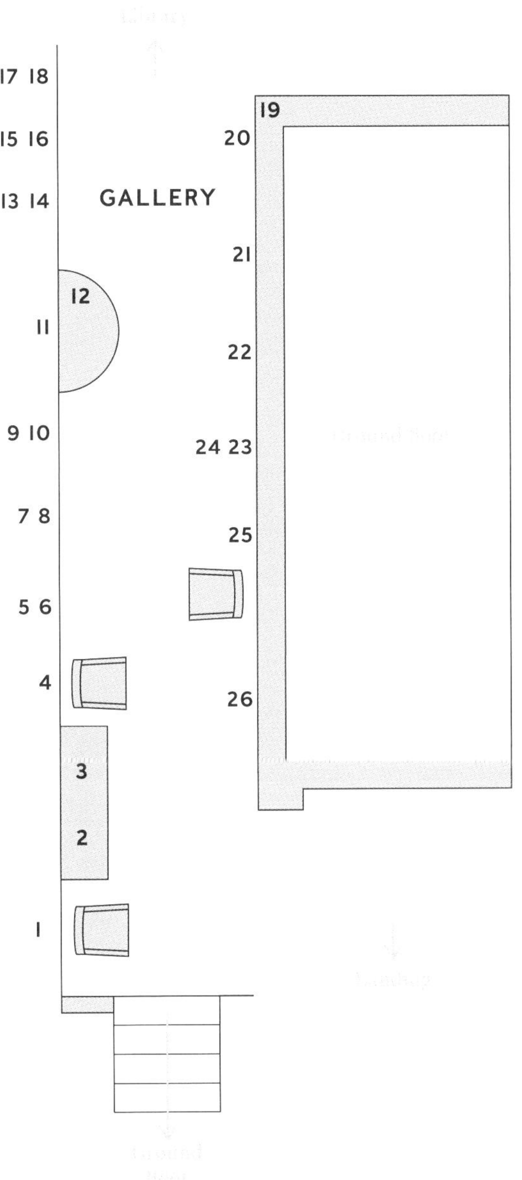

Library
17 18
19
15 16
20
GALLERY
13 14
21
12
11
22
9 10
24 23
7 8
25
5 6
4
26
3
2
1

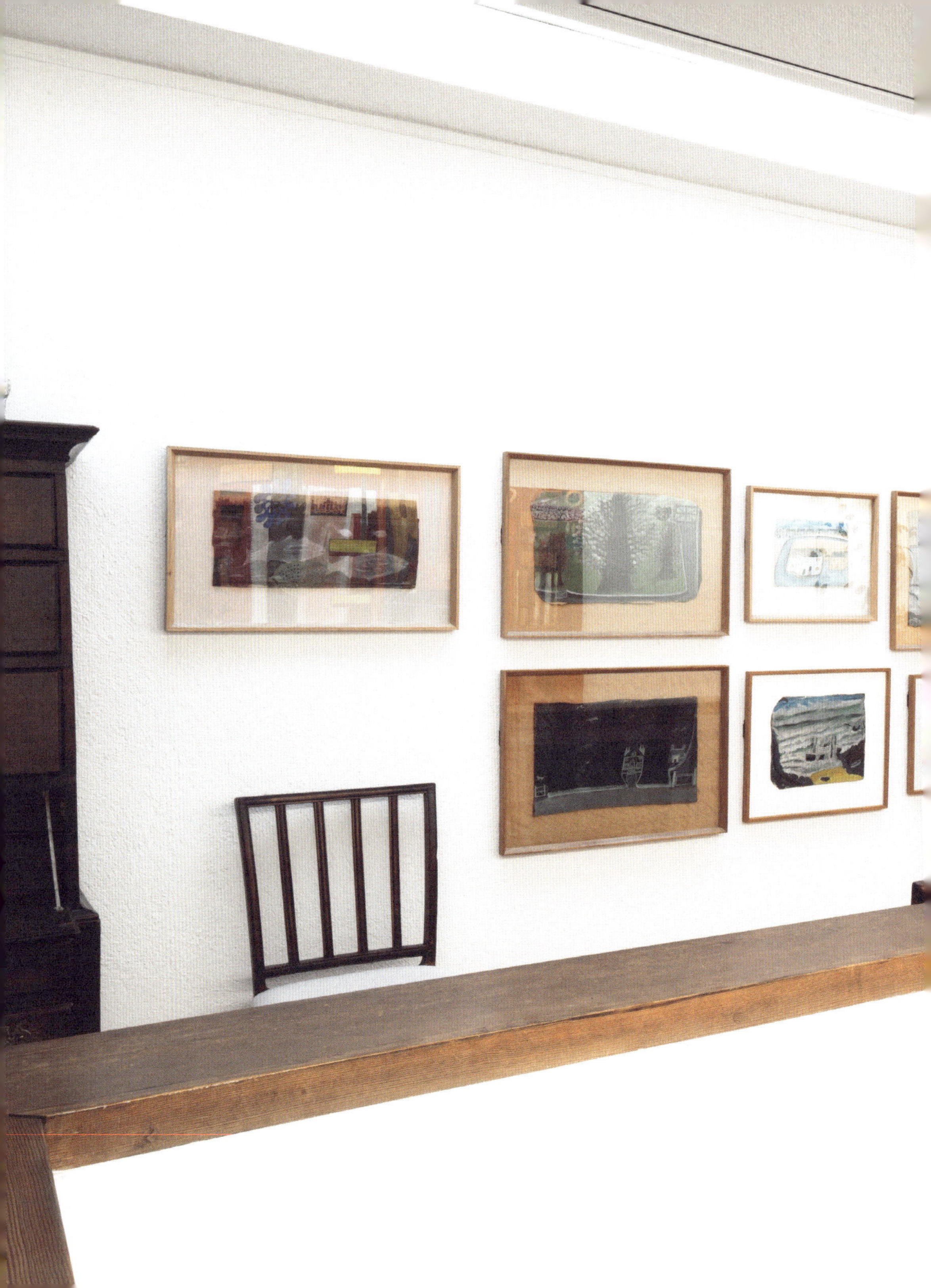

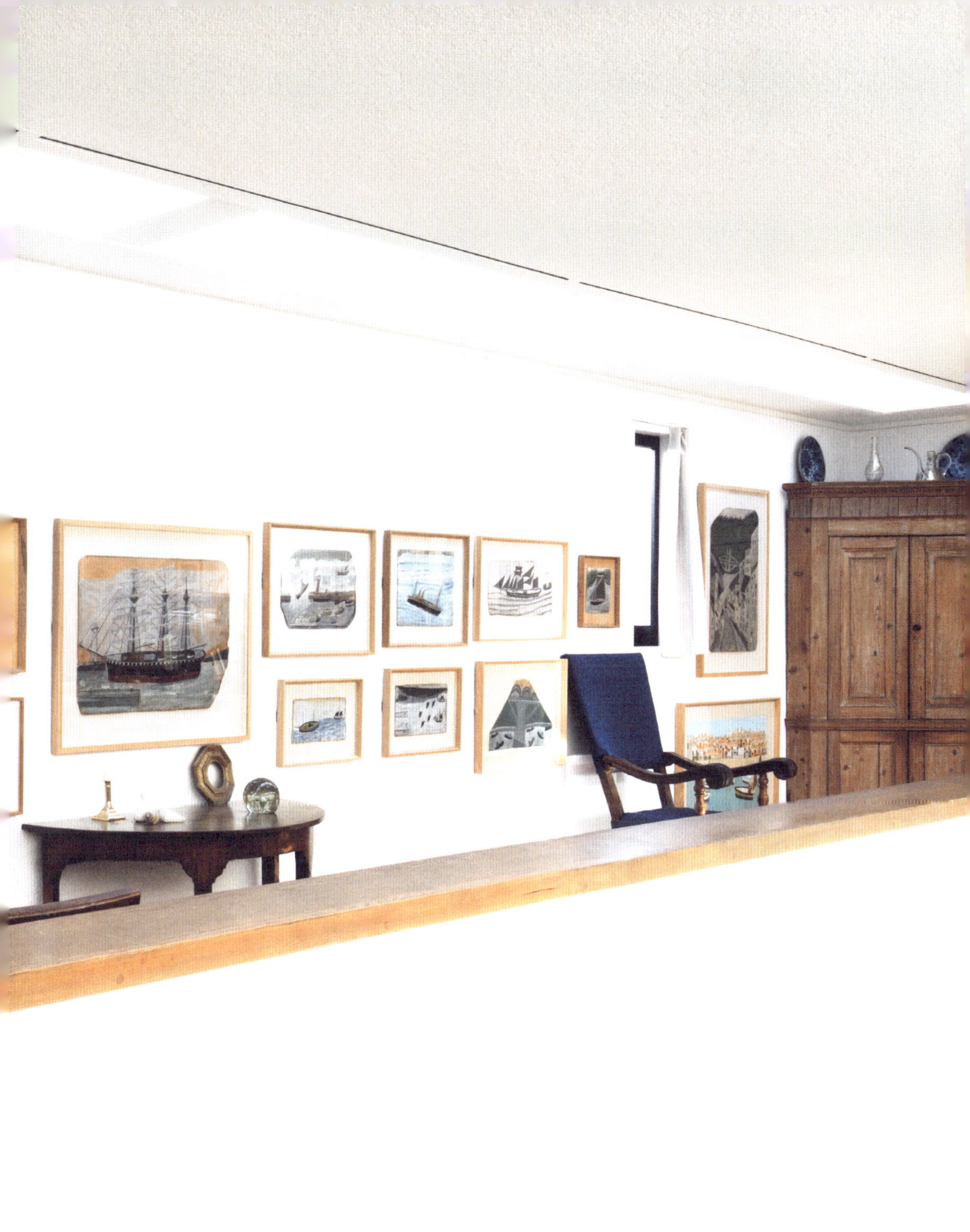

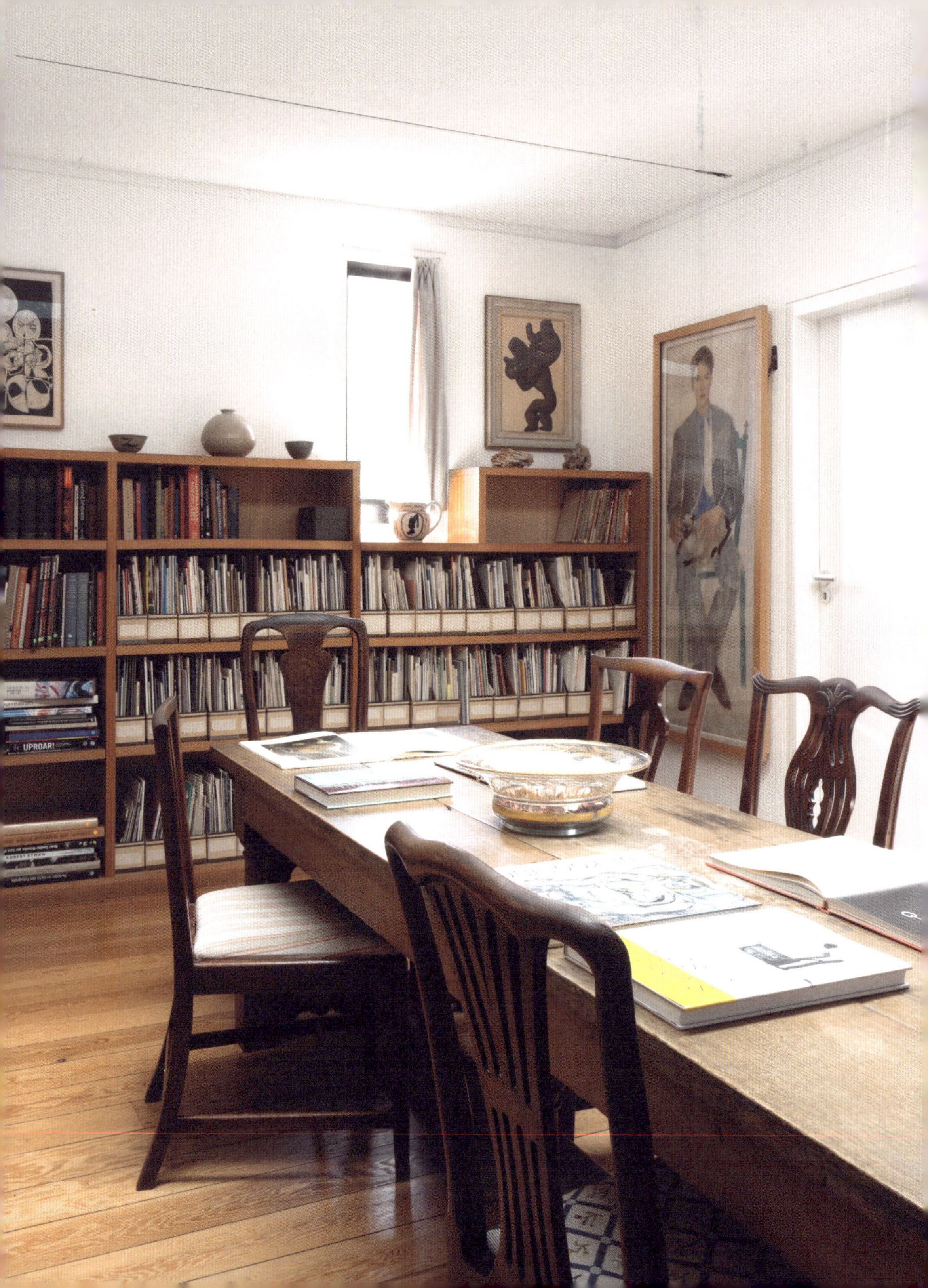
UPROAR!

LIBRARY

The long late seventeenth-century table, around which visitors are invited to sit and read, was salvaged from the kitchen of Clare College, Cambridge. The books - which in this area visitors may take off the shelves - include those collected by the Edes as well as by subsequent curators at Kettle's Yard. On top of the shelves are ceramics given by artists and friends of the Edes, including a jug made by Dorothy Stratford that was given to them by the artist and designer E.Q. Nicholson, pots given to Kettle's Yard that were previously in the collection of Zoë and Jan Ellison, and a more recent gift from Angela Verren Taunt of a mochaware jug that belonged to Ben Nicholson, and features in his painting *1930 (plate, cup and jug)* which hangs on the ground floor. Also atop the Library shelves is a piece of wood burrowed through by marine worms and a piece of quartz crystal. Part of the shelves (under the window) were added in the late 1970s, after the Edes had left Kettle's Yard. The rug next to the table is from present day Turkmenistan and dates from the late nineteenth century. On the mezzanine ledge overlooking the ground floor is a 'hoya carnosa' plant.

1 Alfred Wallis
Sailing ship and orchard, c. 1935–37
Oil paint on card
KY00685.EH

2 Armchair, Spain, late 17th century
Walnut wood
KY00484.EH

3 Alfred Wallis
Saltash (or Devonport), c. 1928–30
Oil paint and watercolour on board
KY00402.EH

4 Bryan Pearce
St Ives Harbour, undated
Oil paint on board
KY01117.EH

5 Two plates, Delft, Netherlands, c. 1760
Porcelain
KY00636a-b.EH

6 Ewer and rosewater sprinkler, Beykoz, Turkey, 19th century
Gilded glass
KY00843.EH
KY00842.EH

7 Corner cupboard, England, 18th century
Wood
KY0955.EH

8 James Dixon
Tory Island, 1966
Oil paint and paper on board
KY00903.EH

9 Henri Gaudier-Brzeska
Boy with uplifted arms, 1913 (cast 1968)
Bronze
KY00934.EH

10 Ben Nicholson
1932-34 (head), 1932–34
Linocut print on card
KY00647.EH

11 Two jelly moulds, 19th and 20th century
Ceramic
KY00192.EH

12 Ben Nicholson
mug, c. 1928
Linocut print on card
KY00622.EH

13 Ben Nicholson
jug and bowl, c. 1928
Linocut print on card
KY00623.EH

14 Goblet (with feathers), c. 1780
Glass
KY00198.EH

15 Fluted dish, late 19th century; remade by David Stonehouse, 2024
Glazed stoneware
KY01424

16 Pan-top bowl, 19th century
Glass
KY00200.EH

17 Ben Nicholson
1934 (abstract design), 1934
Linocut print on paper
KY00716.EH

18 'Moon jug', once belonging to Ben Nicholson (1894–1982)
Mochaware ceramic
KY01431

19 Henri Gaudier-Brzeska
Torso, 1913 (posthumous cast)
Bronze
KY00811.EH

20 William Staite Murray
Vase, c. 1922
Glazed earthenware
KY01363

21 Zoë Ellison
Vase, c. 1955
Glazed stoneware
KY01199

22 Avinash Chandra
Design, 1961
Print and gouache on paper
KY00792.E

23 Studio of Bernard Leach
Bowl, c. 1950
Glazed stoneware
KY01201

24 Katherine Pleydell-Bouverie
Bottle, 1974
Glazed stoneware
KY01160

25 Katherine Pleydell-Bouverie
Bowl, 1974
Glazed stoneware
KY01198

26 Dorothy Stratford
Jug, 1959
Lustreware
KY01112.EH

27 Henri Gaudier-Brzeska
Wrestlers, c. 1914
Graphite and wash on paper
KY00498.EH

28 Christopher Wood
Boy with Cat (Jean Bourgoint), 1926
Oil paint and graphite on canvas
KY01161.EH

29 Dish, Beykoz, Turkey, 19th century
Gilded glass
KY00844.EH

30 Ian Hamilton Finlay,
Poem/Print no. 11, 1969
Silkscreen print on paper
KY00999.EH

31 Alfred Wallis
Cottages in a wood – St Ives, c. 1935–37
Oil paint on card
KY00684.EH

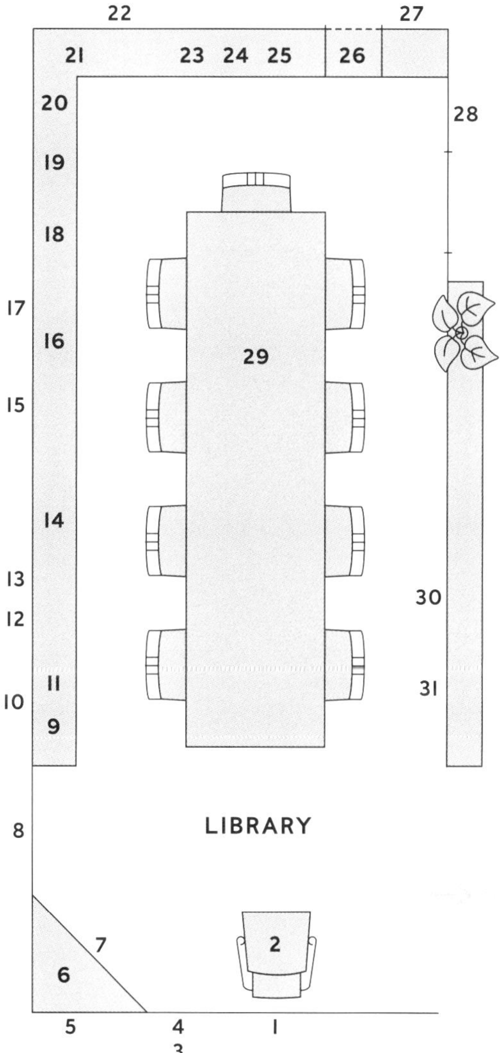
22
27
21
23
24
25
26
20
28
19
18
17
16
29
15
14
13
30
12
11
31
10
9
8
LIBRARY
7
2
6
5
4
3
1

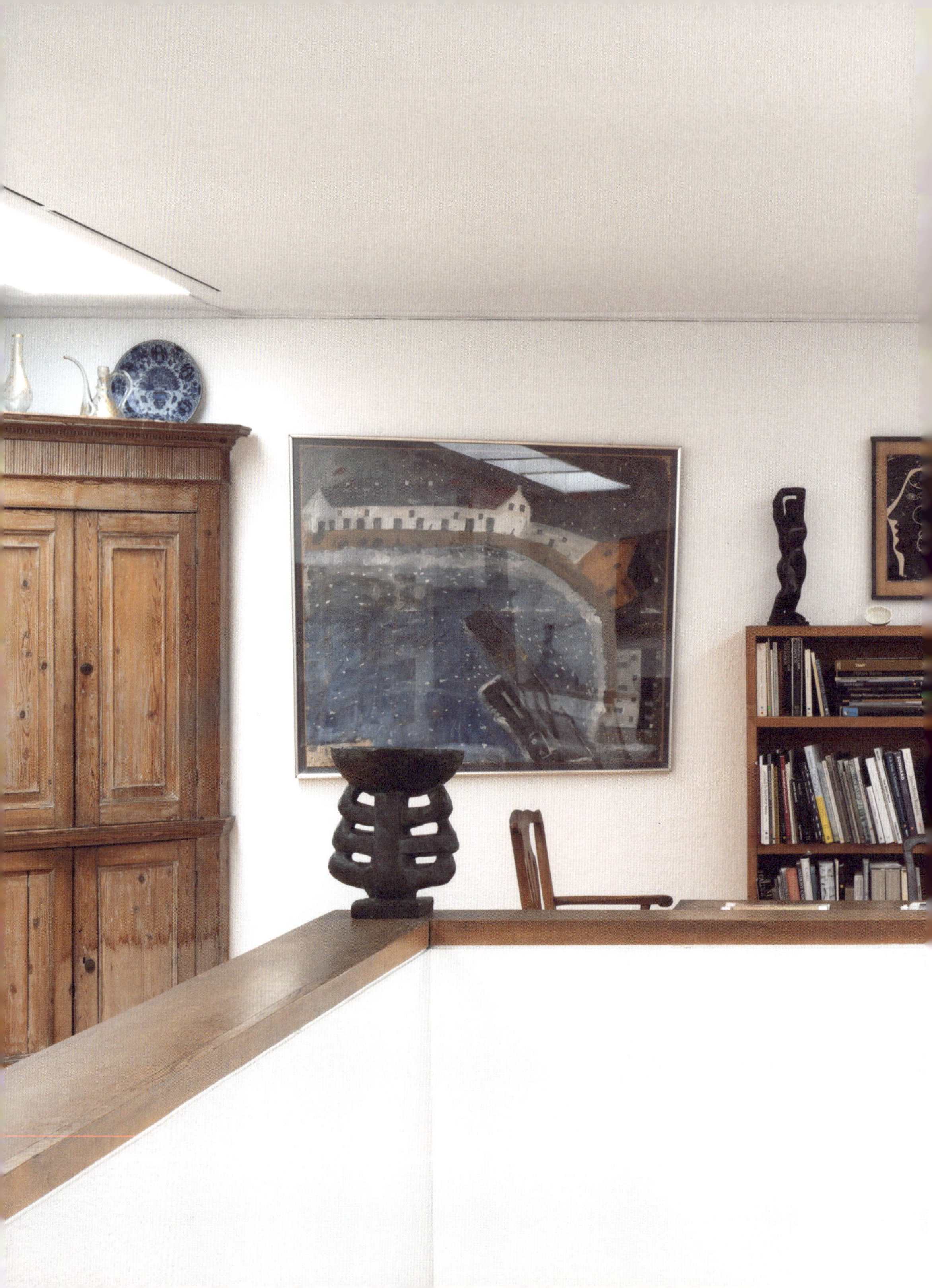

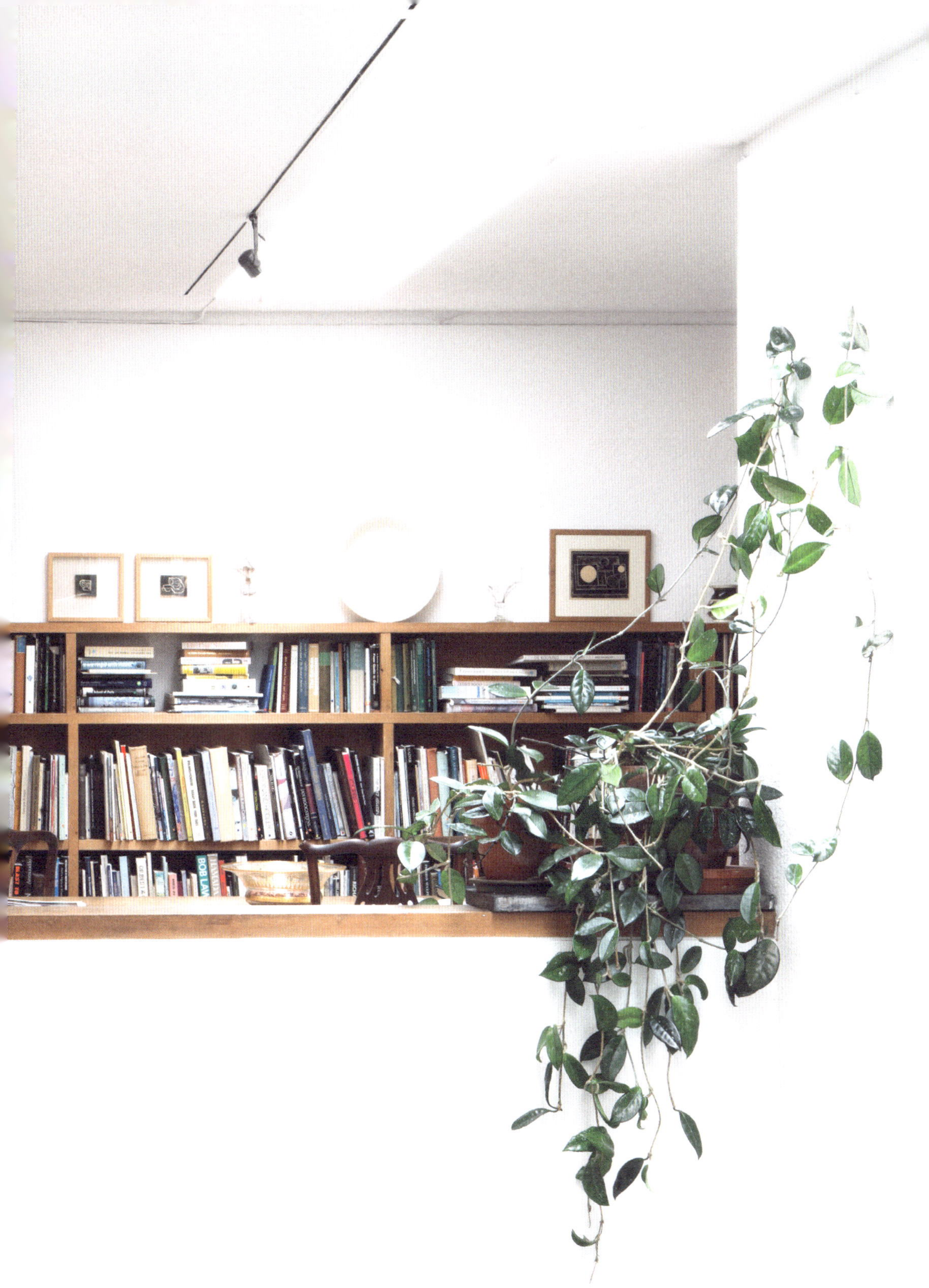
BOB LAW

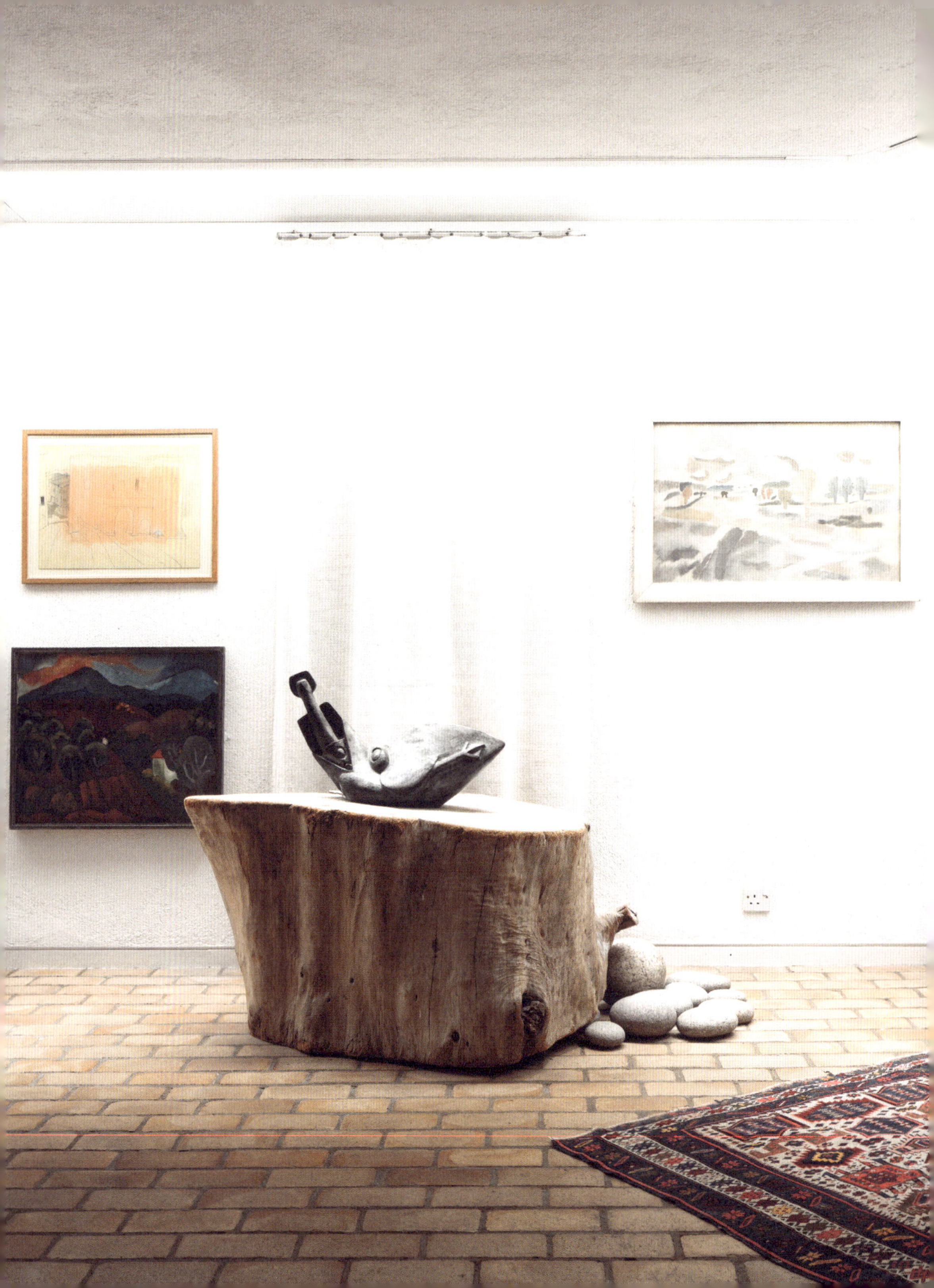

GROUND FLOOR I

Coming down from the upper floor, the area to the left of the staircase contains works by the artists the Edes were closest to in the 1920s - David Jones, Ben and Winifred Nicholson and Christopher Wood. The striking base for Henri Gaudier-Brzeska's *Bird Swallowing a Fish* is part of a tree that Jim Ede found washed up on the beach in the Isles of Scilly in 1966. He initially gave it to Barbara Hepworth to store it in her studio in nearby St Ives, hinting in letters that he hoped she might make a sculpture especially for it. However, when placing works for Kettle's Yard's new spaces, Jim Ede wrote to Hepworth and asked for it to be returned. Christopher Wood's *Building the Boat, Tréboul* is one of several paintings by the artist that Ede acquired following Wood's death. Ede assisted the artist's parents at this time and helped stage a memorial exhibition at the Lefevre Galleries in 1932. Under the large chest of drawers, is a nineteenth-century Kuba rug from the East Caucasus region. A rug from present day Turkmenistan lies next to the low slate shelf. A silk batik from Bali, sent to Jim Ede by the artist Ian Fairweather, originally hung on the staircase wall, but is now in storage for conservation reasons. The pomander is one of two given by the arts patron and society hostess, Lady Ottoline Morrell (1873-1938), who Ede knew through their work together at the Contemporary Art Society.

1 David Jones
Quia per Incarnati, c. 1953
Watercolour and graphite on paper
KY00766.EH

2 Ben Nicholson
1925 (bottle and goblet), 1925
Oil paint on board
KY00331.EH

3 Bible box, England, 17th century
Carved oak
KY01092.EH

4 Ben Nicholson
1929 (Kingwater Valley, Cumberland), 1929
Pencil and oil paint on canvas
KY01426

5 Kate Nicholson
Isle of Skye, 1948
Oil paint on canvas
KY00758.EH

or (verso) Winifred Nicholson
Portrait of a Lady, undated
Oil paint on canvas

6 Henri Gaudier-Brzeska
Seated Woman, 1914 (cast 1964)
Bronze
KY00874.EH

7 Christopher Wood
Building the Boat, Tréboul, 1930
Oil paint on board
KY00630.EH

8 Pomander, 20th century
Orange and cloves
KY00377.EH

9 Tun shell, undated
KY00376.EH

10 Ben Nicholson
1927 (snowscape), 1927
Oil paint on canvas
KY00335.EH

11 Part of a tree, found 1966
KY00912.EH

12 Henri Gaudier-Brzeska
Bird Swallowing a Fish, 1914
Painted plaster
KY00493.EH

13 Ben Nicholson
1955 (spello), 1955
Graphite and watercolour on card
KY00763.EH

14 Christopher Wood
Landscape at Vence - Little White House, 1927
Oil paint on canvas
KY00339.EH

15 Henri Gaudier-Brzeska
Birds Erect, 1914 (posthumous cast)
Cast stone
KY00985.EH

16 Large glass goblet, undated
KY01084.EH

17 Lucie Rie
Bowl, c. 1971–74
Ceramic
KY01140.EH

18 Sandstone with fish fossil, undated
KY01105.EH

19 L.S. Lowry
Mountain Lake, 1943
Oil paint on board
KY00986.EH

20 Henri Gaudier-Brzeska
Head of Mlle Borne, 1914 (posthumous cast)
Bronze
KY01276.EH

21 Winifred Nicholson
Cyclamen and Primula, c. 1923
Oil paint on board
KY00767.EH

22 Winifred Nicholson
Seascape (Sea and Sand), 1926
Oil paint on canvas
KY00387.EH

23 Winifred Nicholson
Sam Graves, c. 1930
Oil paint on board
KY00674.EH

24 Henri Gaudier-Brzeska
Three Monkeys, 1914
Sandstone
KY00487.EH

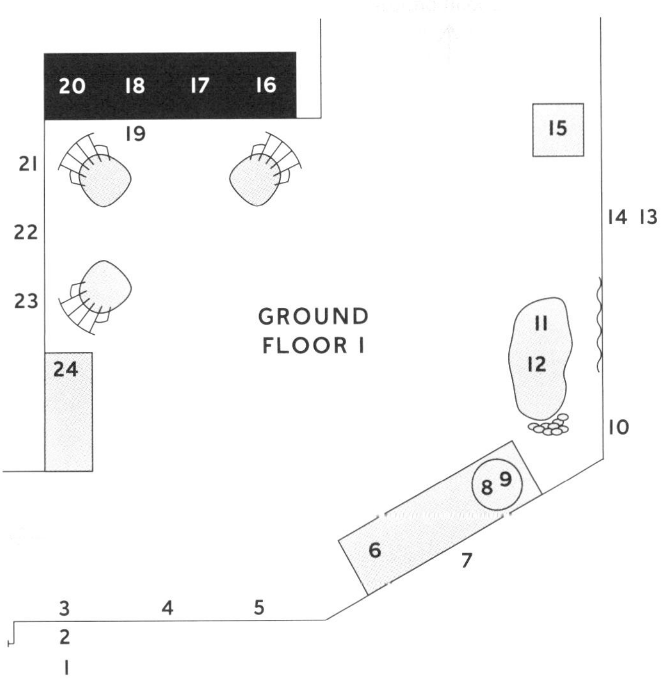
20
18
17
16
19
15
21
22
14
13
23
GROUND
FLOOR 1
11
12
24
10
8
9
6
7
3
4
5
2
1

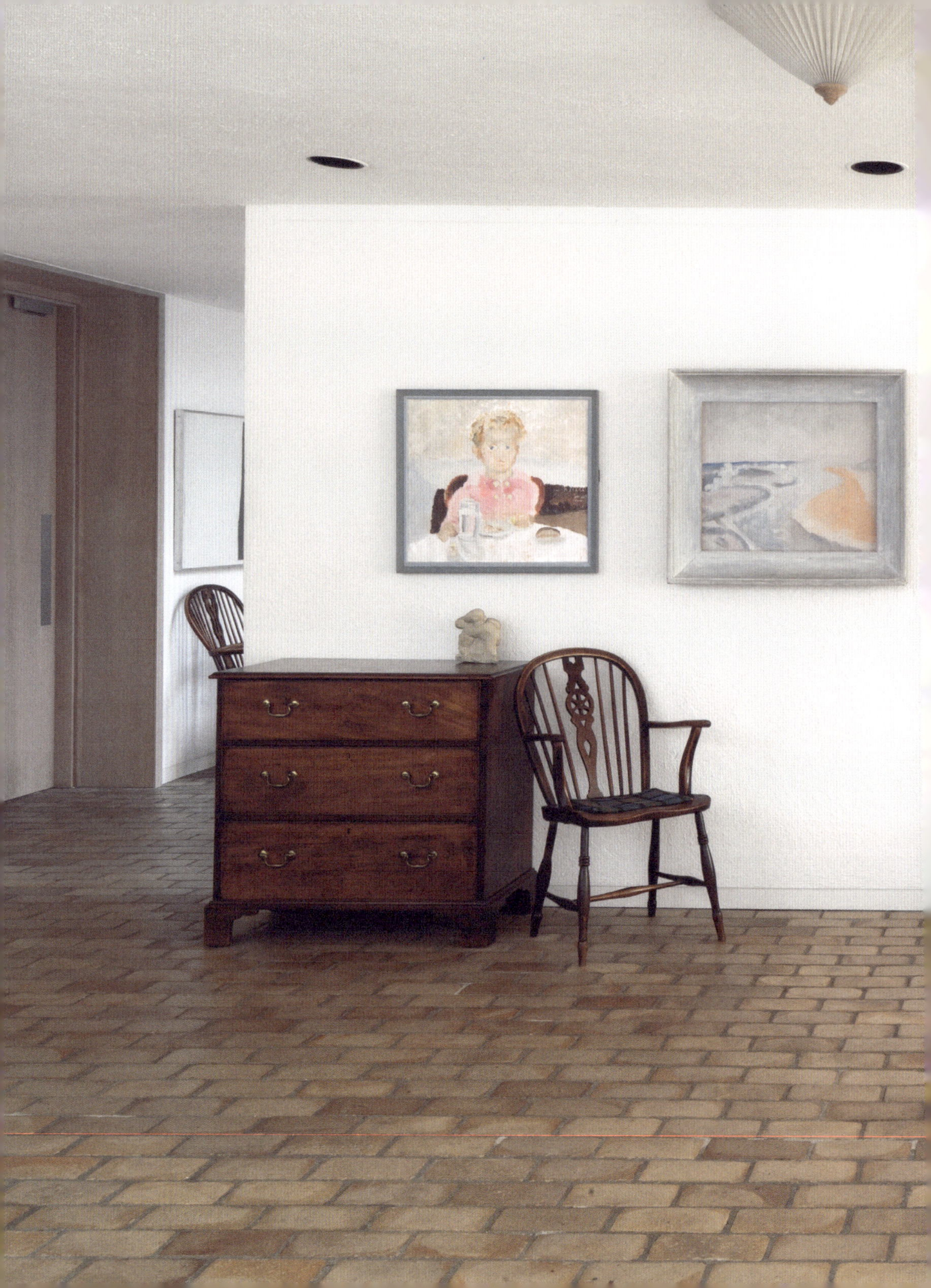

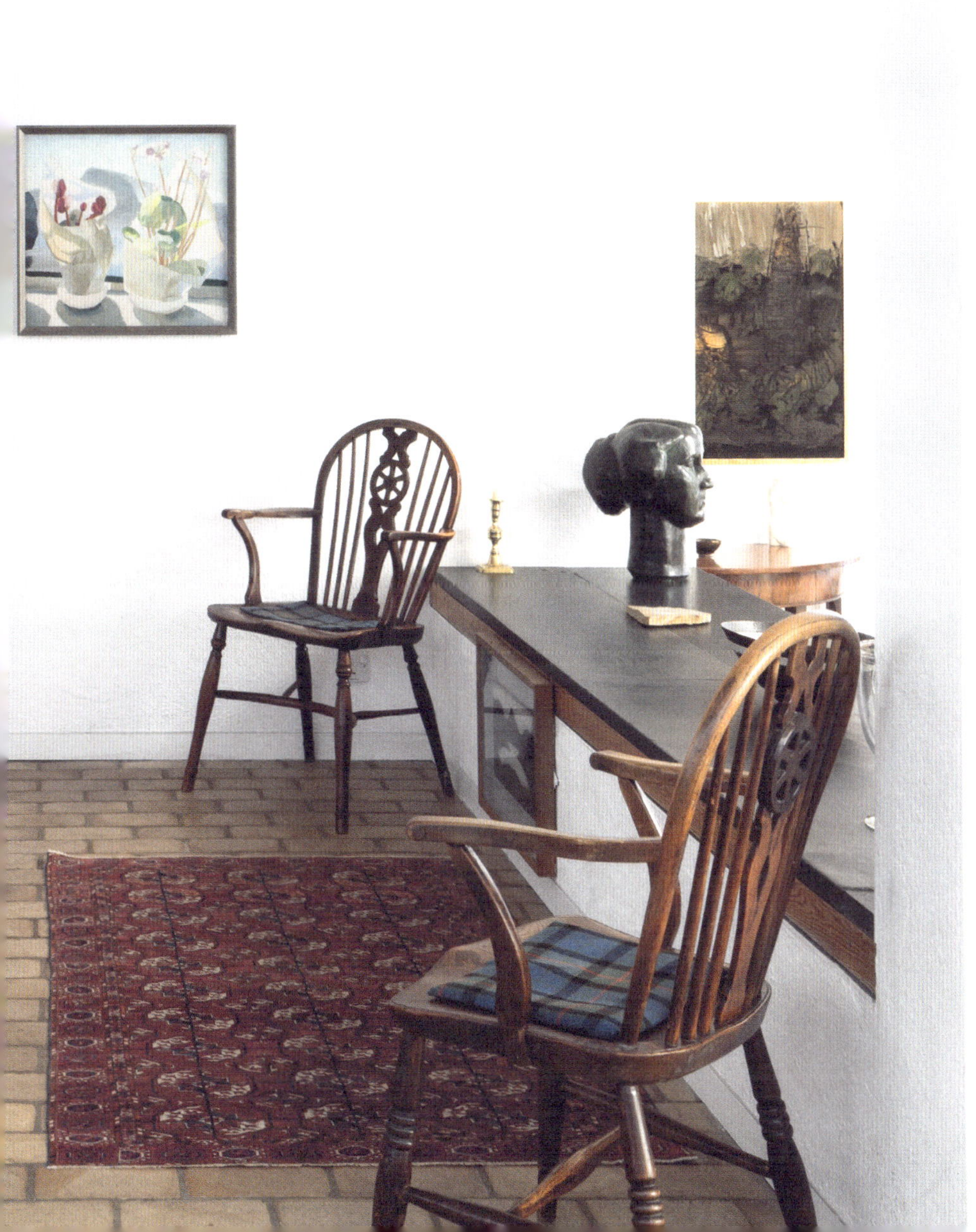

GROUND FLOOR 2

The area leading down via the steps and ramp includes works by Ben Nicholson and Henri Gaudier-Brzeska. The altar-like table was made from wood taken from a shed that was dismantled during the building of the 1970 extension. On either end are sculptures by Henri Gaudier-Brzeska, and above are paintings by Ben Nicholson and Alfred Wallis. The rug in front was made in the South-West Caucasus region. A 'schefflera elegantissima' plant is sometimes found next to the Khmer Buddha (seated on the Nāga King), which was purchased by Jim Ede in 1970 and placed on three roughly hewn octagonal sections of wood that were among those items salvaged from the Clare College kitchens.

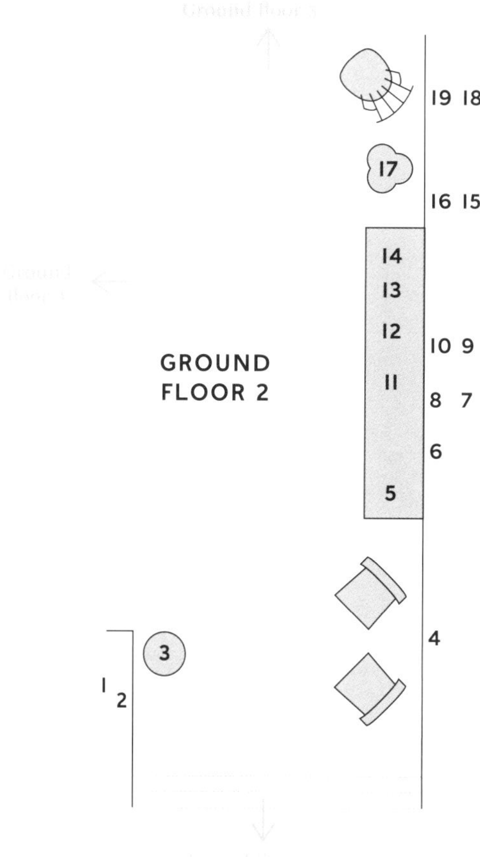

1 Ben Nicholson
1924 June (Balearic Isles), 1924
Oil paint and graphite on canvas
KY00336.EH

2 Ben Nicholson
circa 1933 (exhibition sign), c. 1933
Oil paint on linoleum
KY00646.EH

3 Henri Gaudier-Brzeska
Red Stone Dancer, 1913–14 (cast 1969)
Bronze
KY00984.EH

4 Henri Gaudier-Brzeska
Lady Macbeth poster, 1912
Gouache on paper
KY00497.EH

5 Henri Gaudier-Brzeska
Maternity (Mother and Child), 1913 (cast 1960s)
Bronze
KY00809.EH

6 Ben Nicholson
1924 (Bertha no. 2), 1924
Oil paint and graphite on canvas
KY00330.EH

7 Ben Nicholson
1930 (plate, cup and jug), 1930
Oil paint and graphite on board
KY00645.EH

8 Ben Nicholson
1962 (argos), 1962
Oil paint and carved board on wood
KY00853.EH

9 Ben Nicholson
1924 (goblet and two pears), 1924
Oil paint and graphite on board
KY00337.EH

10 Alfred Wallis
Small boat in a rough sea, c. 1936
Oil paint on card
KY00692.EH

11 Bowl, Crete, c. 2700 BCE
Terracotta
KY00848.EH

12 Incised bowl, Crete, c. 2700 BCE
Terracotta
KY00847.EH

13 Three quartz geodes, undated
KY00196.EH

14 Henri Gaudier-Brzeska
Garden Ornament 2, 1914 (posthumous cast)
Bronze
KY00817.EH

15 Mario Sironi
Drawing for reliefs (six half-length figures), c. 1940s
Conté crayon and charcoal on paper
KY01020.EH

16 Henri Gaudier-Brzeska
Woman and Dog, 1914
Charcoal on paper
KY00503.EH

17 Khmer Buddha from Phra Prang Sam Yot temple, Lopburi, Thailand, c. 13–14th century
Stone
KY01023.EH

18 Italo Valenti
Veneti, 1962–64
Paper collage on board
KY00918.EH

19 Ben Nicholson
1928 (three mugs and a bowl), 1928
Linocut on paper
KY00621.EH

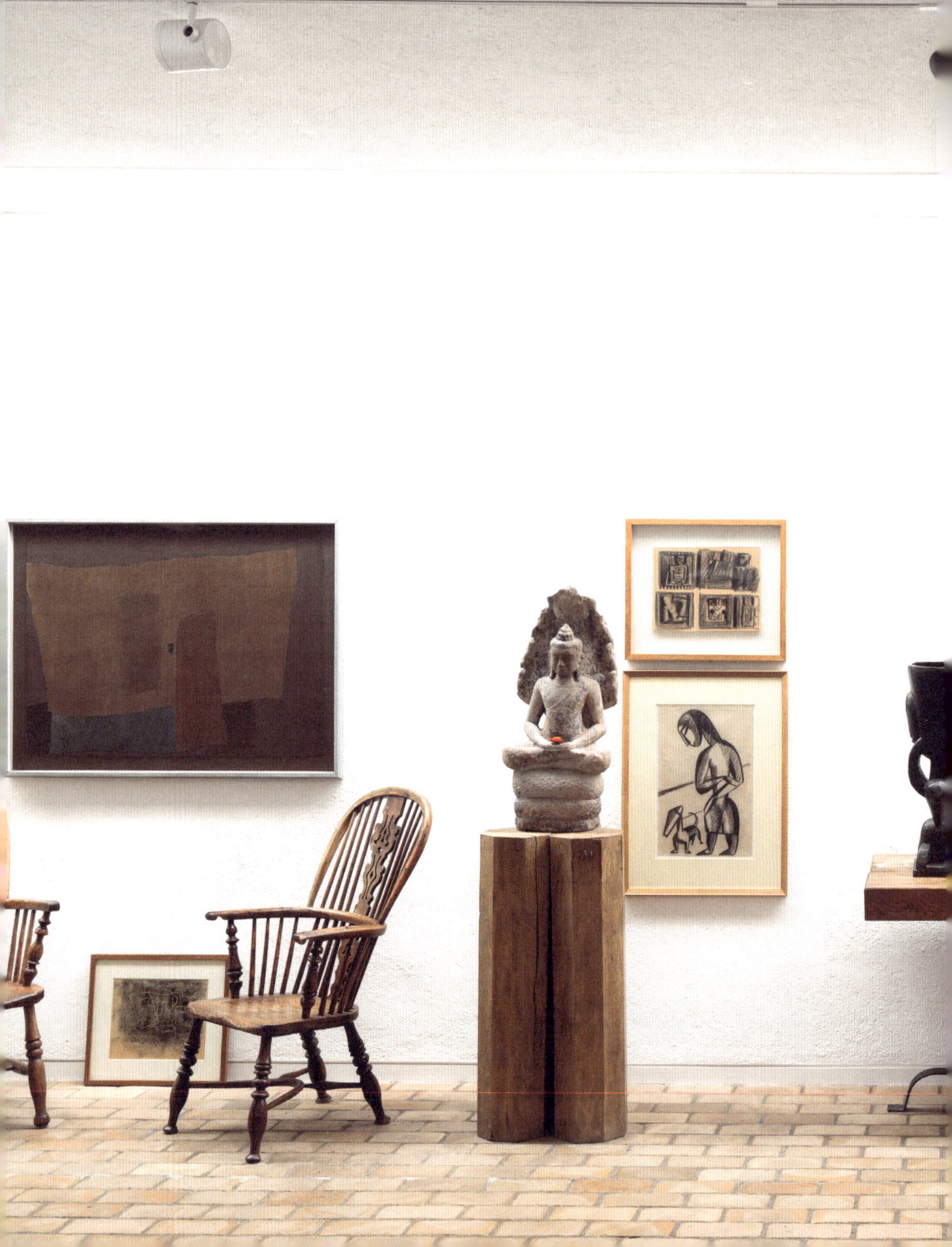

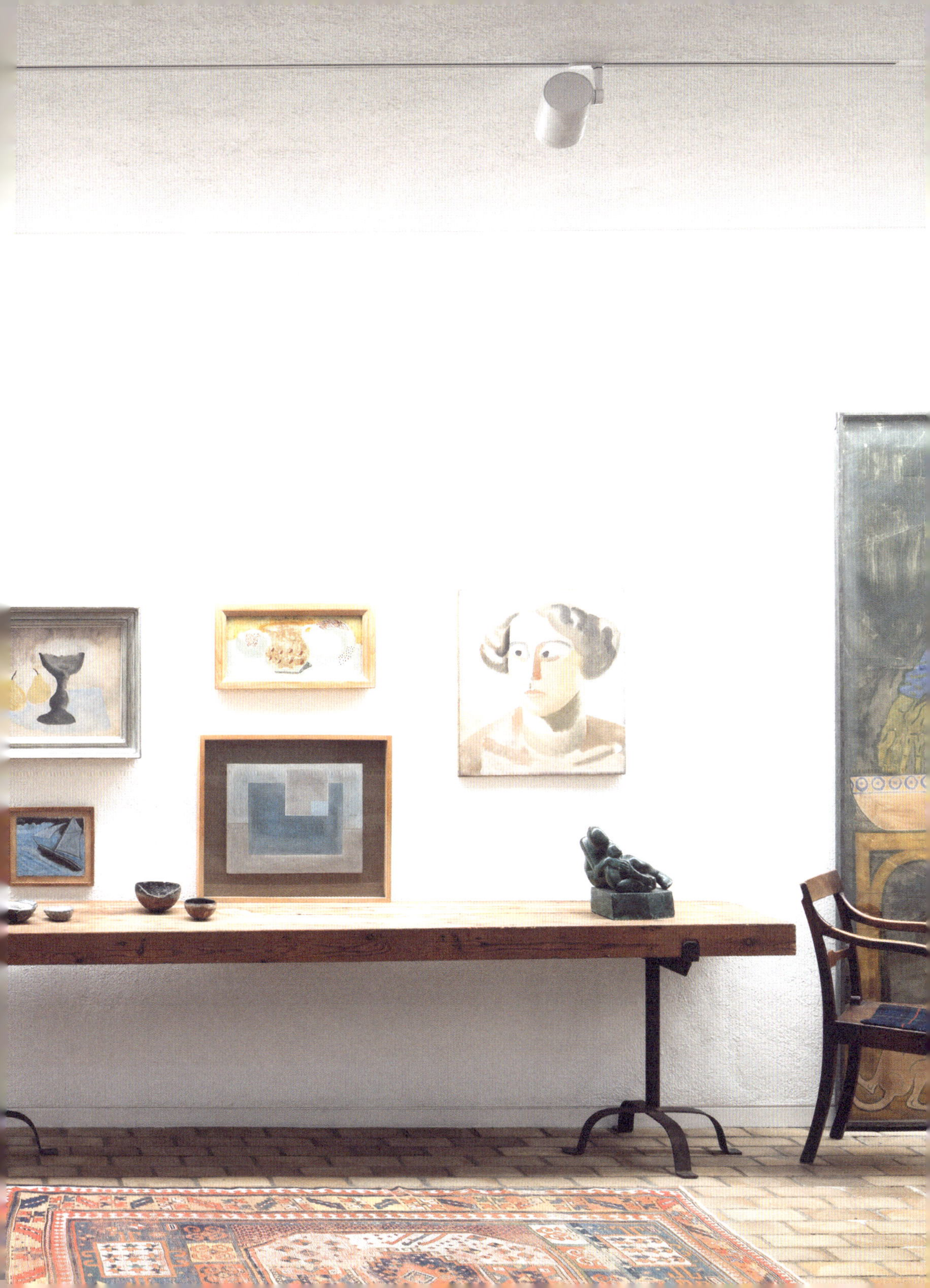

GROUND FLOOR 3

This area of the house was originally designed as a 'green room' for musicians performing at Kettle's Yard, and the tracks for the concealed door to partition this space are still visible. The slate table against the wall holds glassware, found objects and a bowl by Lucie Rie. Above are three large black and white works by Italo Valenti and a shelf of nineteenth-century porcelain. A low bookcase nearby holds several titles by the writer T.E. Lawrence (1888–1935), who Jim Ede wrote to from 1927 and met on several occasions. In 1942 Ede published a book of their correspondence.

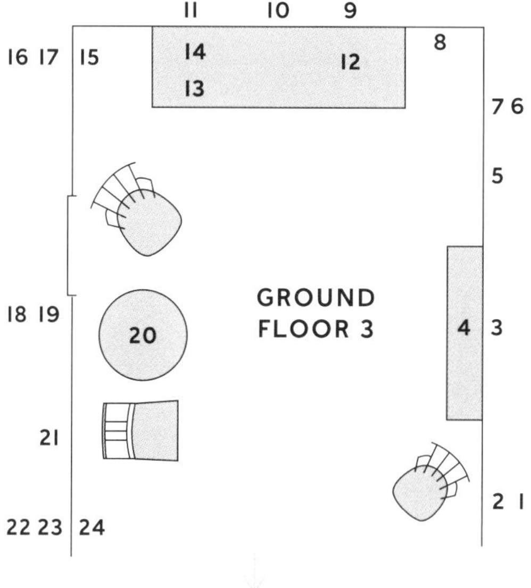

1 Roger Hilton
January 1961 (Black and Brown on White), 1961
Oil paint on canvas
KY00855.EH

2 Edmond Xavier Kapp
Design, 1965
Wash paint on paper
KY00806.EH

3 Christopher Wood
Self Portrait, 1927
Oil paint on canvas
KY00338.EH

4 Head of a two-pronged hoe, 19th century
Metal
KY00193.EH

5 Ben Nicholson
1933 (profiles), 1933
Linocut print on paper
KY00702.EH

6 John Lyons
Whip Snake, 2007
Woodcut print on paper
KY01406

7 Frank Auerbach
R.B. Kitaj, 1980
Etching on paper
KY01215

8 Jug, Cyprus, c. 700 BCE
Earthenware
KY00846.EH

9 Italo Valenti
Nr. 286; Pietra; Pierre, 1964
Paper collage on hardboard
KY00878.EH

10 Italo Valenti
Nr. 287; Giardino a mezzogiorno; Jardin à midi, 1964
Paper collage on hardboard
KY00877.EH

11 Italo Valenti
Nr. 284; Etana, 1964
Paper collage on hardboard
KY00876.EH

12 Lucie Rie
Conical Bowl, 1971
Glazed stoneware
KY01130.EH

13 John Clegg
Fiddle Fish, 1963
Marble and string
KY00856.EH

14 Three cross-sections of agate stone, undated
KY00191

15 Henri Gaudier-Brzeska
Horace Brodzky Mask, 1913 (cast 1965)
Cast stone
KY01155.E

16 Ben Nicholson
circa 1928 (jug and two mugs), c. 1928
Linocut print on paper
KY00620.EH

17 Bryan Illsley
White Relief, 1966
White cardboard on paper
KY00931.EH

18 Jirí Kolár
Words in Music, c. 1966
Collage, newspaper cuttings on paper
KY01134.E

19 Cecil Collins
The Years, 1937
Ink and wash on paper
KY00648.EH

20 Henri Gaudier-Brzeska
Seated Fawn, 1913 (cast 1920s)
Bronze
KY00371.EH

21 Ben Nicholson
princess (kings and queens), c. 1933
Linocut print on cloth
KY00708.EH

22 Naum Gabo
Opus 5 (The Constellations), 1950
Monoprint on paper
KY00777.EH

23 Marino Marini
Rider on a Horse, c. 1957
Etched Indian ink wash on paper
KY00987.EH

24 Henri Gaudier-Brzeska
Two Men with a Bowl, 1913-14 (cast c. 1965)
Bronze
KY00898.EH

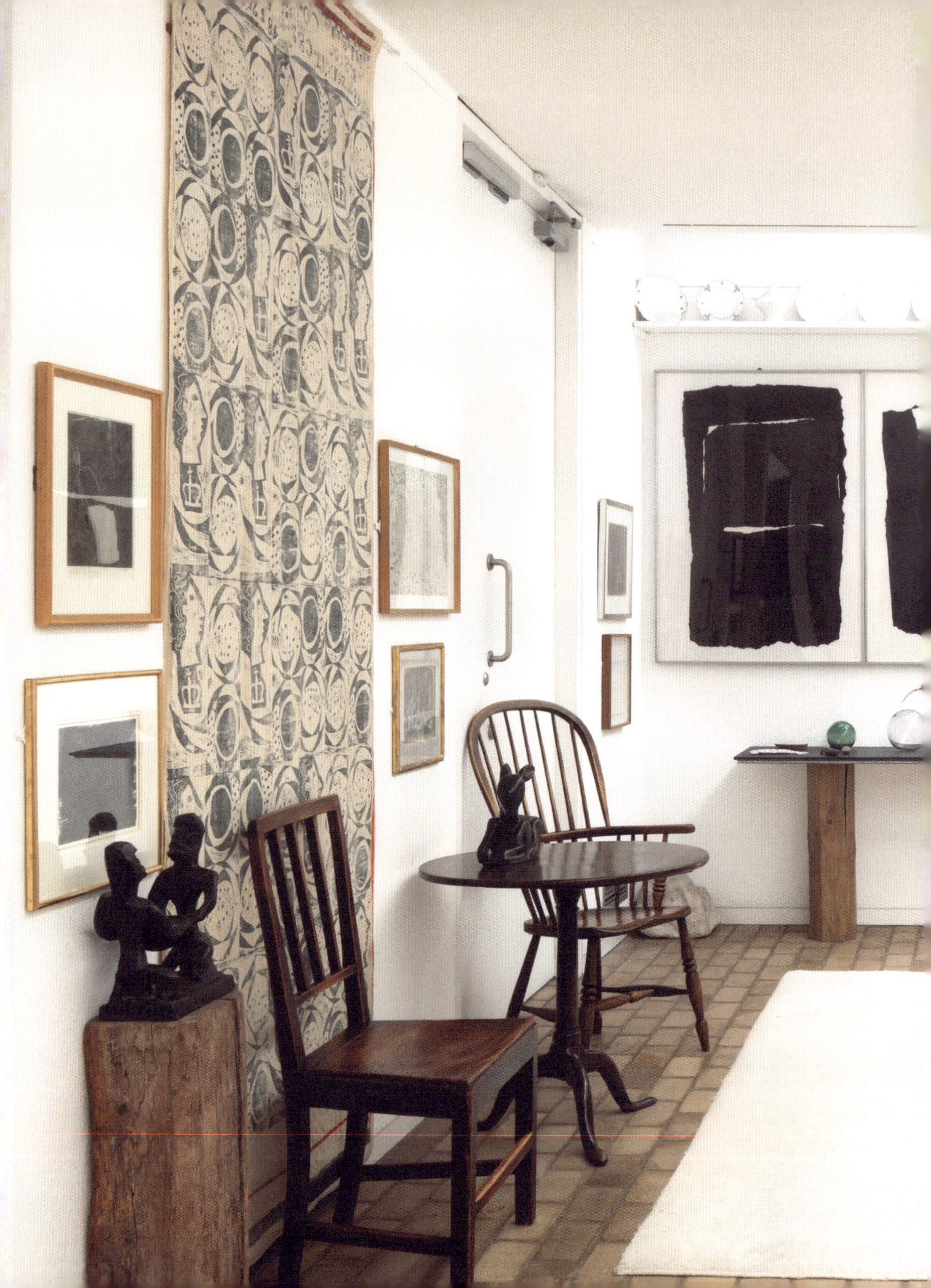

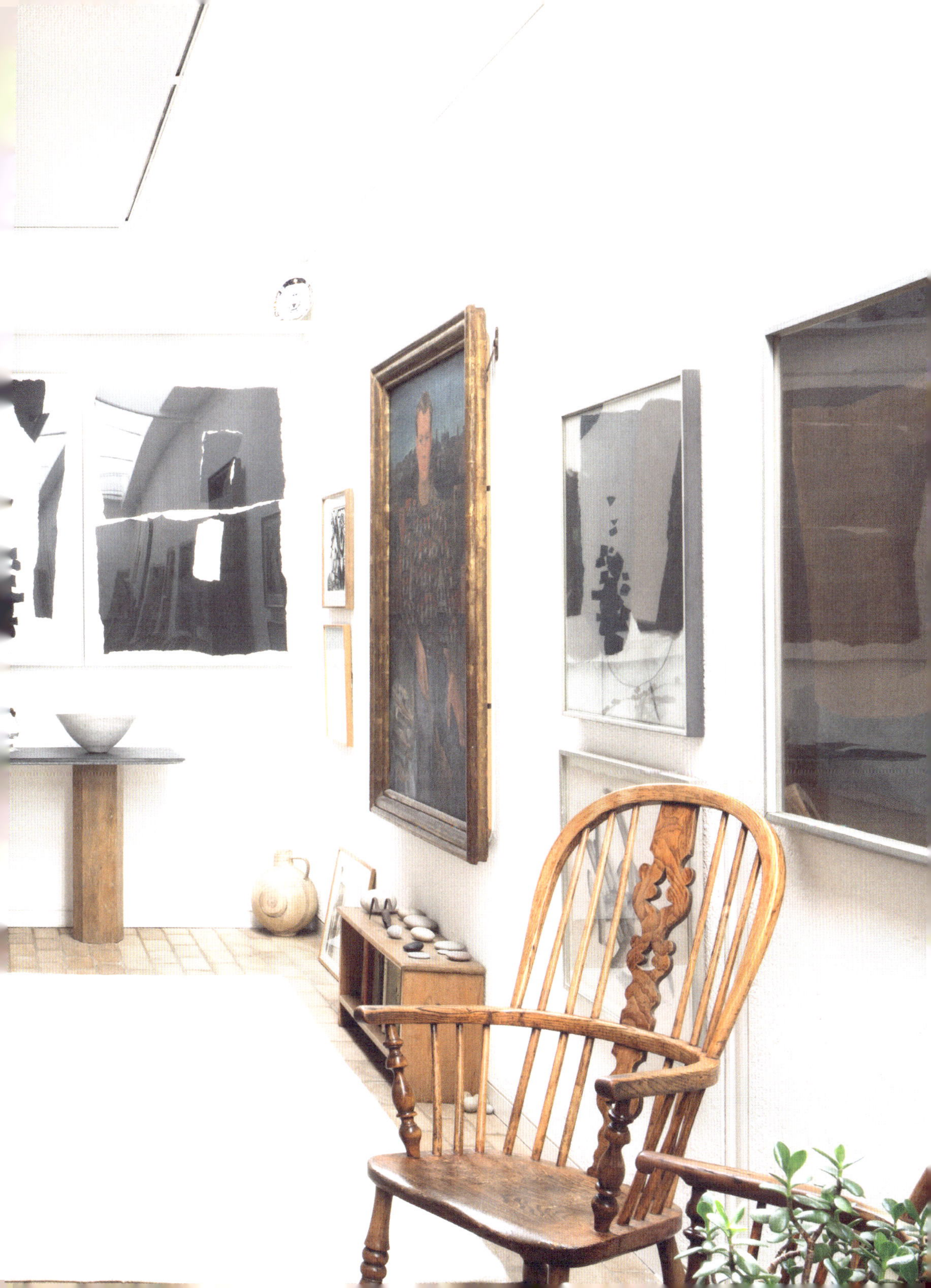

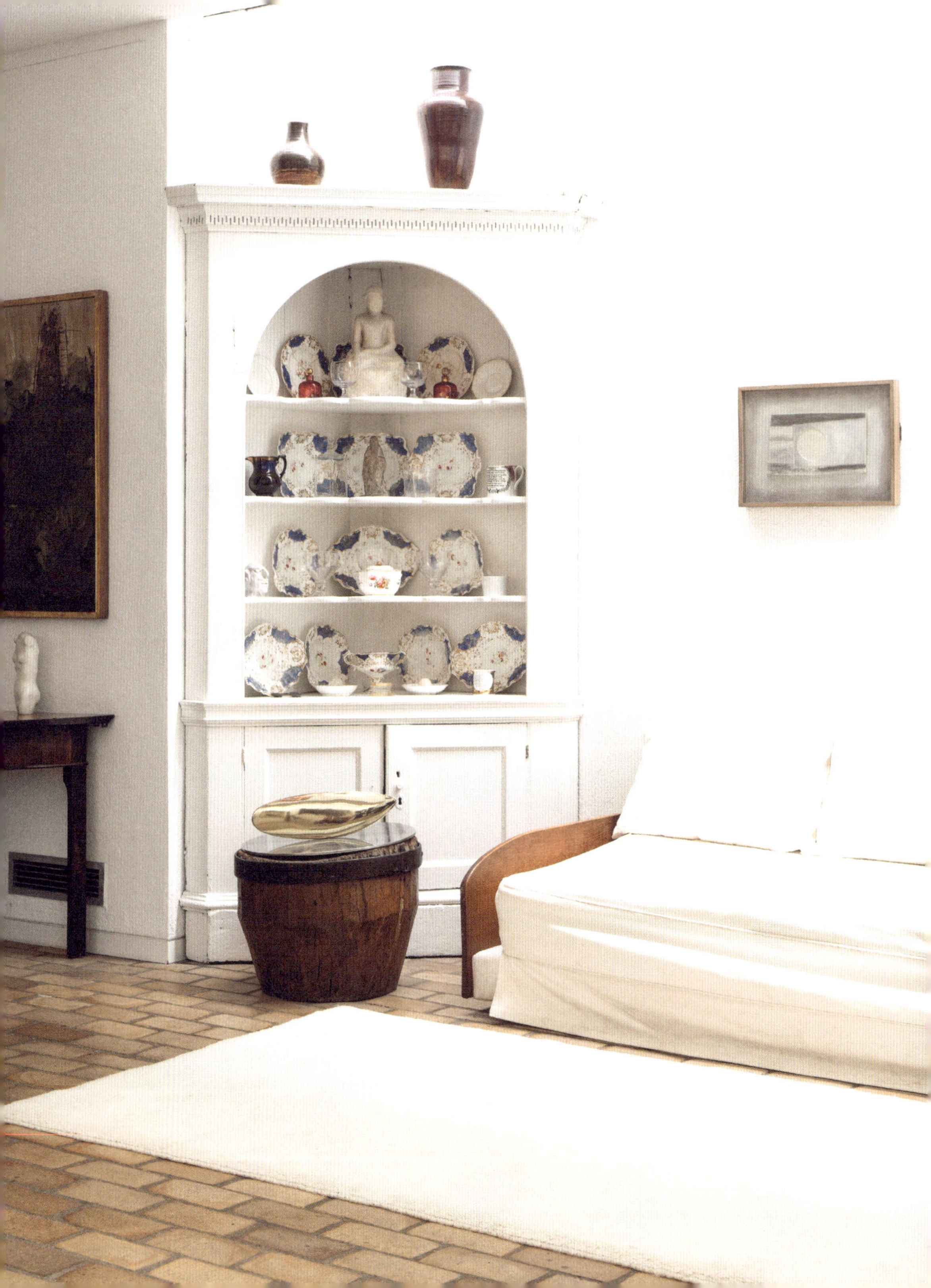

GROUND FLOOR 4

On the ground floor stands a Steinway grand piano which is regularly used for performances. When not in use, the piano carries one of two sculptures by Naum Gabo. Seating in this space includes eighteenth-century Windsor and mahogany 'carver' chairs, a long divan sofa and several twentieth-century Danish beechwood chairs with linen seats and leather arms. Works of art by Ben Nicholson, Alfred Wallis and Winston McQuoid are gathered near the eighteenth-century bureau. Among the small sculptures in the white-painted corner cabinet is a set of blue and white Spode porcelain (c. 1833–47) that was made for Trinity College, Cambridge and purchased by Jim Ede in the twenties. The cabinet also houses other miscellaneous items including two nineteenth-century pink scent bottles made in Bohemia (now part of the Czech Republic), lustreware cups and jug, a small glass salt cellar (c. 1795) and a pestle and mortar.

1 Henri Gaudier-Brzeska
Wrestlers relief, 1913 (cast 1965)
Herculite
KY00896.EH

2 Naum Gabo
Linear Construction in Space No. 1, 1944–45
Perspex and nylon thread
KY00988.EH

or Naum Gabo
Construction in Space: Suspended, 1962
Perspex, nylon thread, acrylic paint and steel
KY01350

3 Ben Nicholson
1933 (musical instruments), 1933
Oil paint on canvas
KY00644.EH

4 George Kennethson
Forms, c.1968
Staffordshire alabaster
KY00942.EH

5 Ben Nicholson
Sept' 55 (Monte Oliveto), 1955
Pencil and oil paint on carved relief board
KY01427

6 Ben Nicholson
1965 (Kos – project for freestanding relief wall), 1965
Oil paint on carved board
KY01428

7 William Staite Murray
Vase, c. 1930
Glazed terracotta
KY01116.EH

8 William Staite Murray
Vase, c. 1930
Glazed terracotta
KY00640.EH

9 Mandalay Buddha, 18th century
Marble
KY00065

10 Henri Gaudier-Brzeska
Figure, 1914
Alabaster
KY00495.EH

11 Henri Gaudier-Brzeska
Head, c. 1912
Glazed ceramic
KY00496.EH

12 Gregorio Vardanega
Small Sphere, c. 1956
Plexiglass
KY00893.EH

13 Constantin Brâncusi
Fish, 1924 (cast 1973)
Brass and steel
KY01151.EH

14 William Congdon
Sri Rangam Temple, Tiruchirapalli (Sri Rangam, Tiruchirapalli), 1954
Oil paint, gold paint and enamel paint on hardboard
KY00772.EH

15 Henri Gaudier-Brzeska
Female Torso, 1913 (cast 1976)
Cast resin and marble
KY01180.EH

16 Bowl, China, Song dynasty
Glazed terracotta and gold
KY01291

17 Henri Gaudier-Brzeska
Woman Carrying Sacks, 1912–13, (cast 1964)
Bronze
KY00875.EH

18 Alfred Wallis
Old Arch Digey (St Ives), undated
Oil paint on card
KY00451.EH

19 Winston McQuoid
Waterfall in the Glen, 1927
Oil paint on plywood
KY00381.EH

20 Ben Nicholson
Porta-San Gimignano, 1953
Etching on paper
KY00849.EH

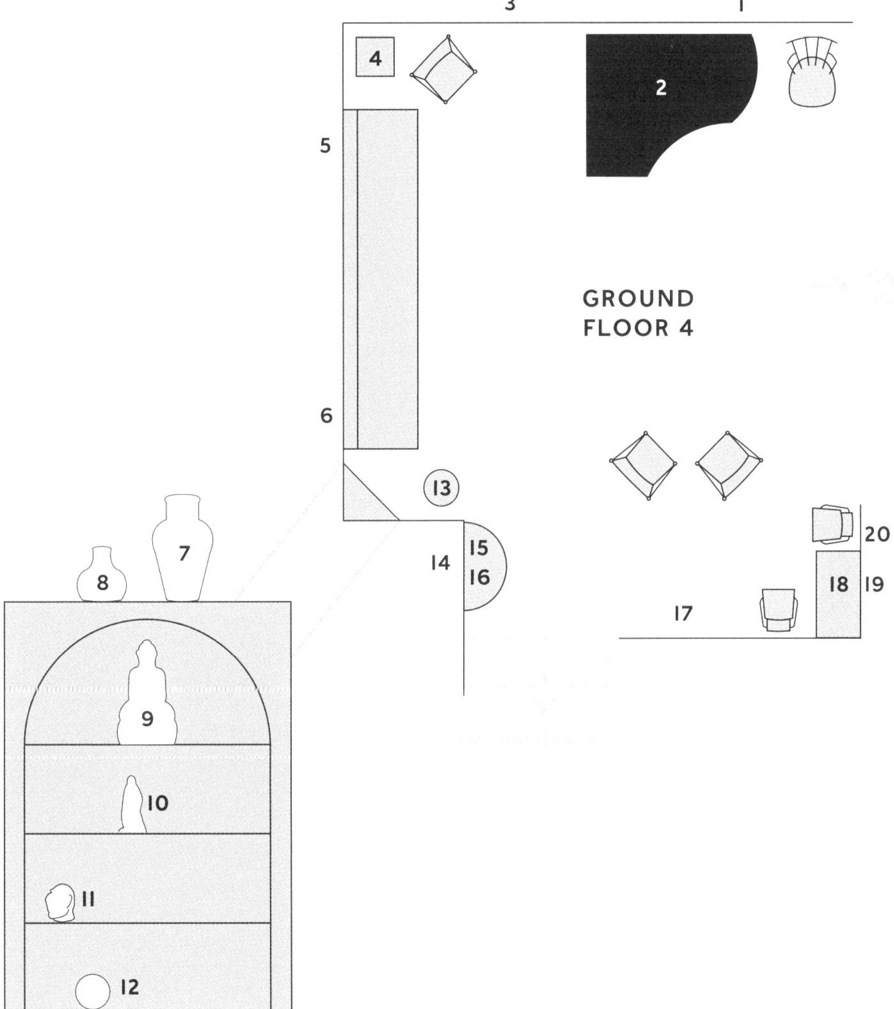
3
1
4
2
5
GROUND
FLOOR 4
6
13
7
8
14
15
16
20
18
19
17
9
10
11
12

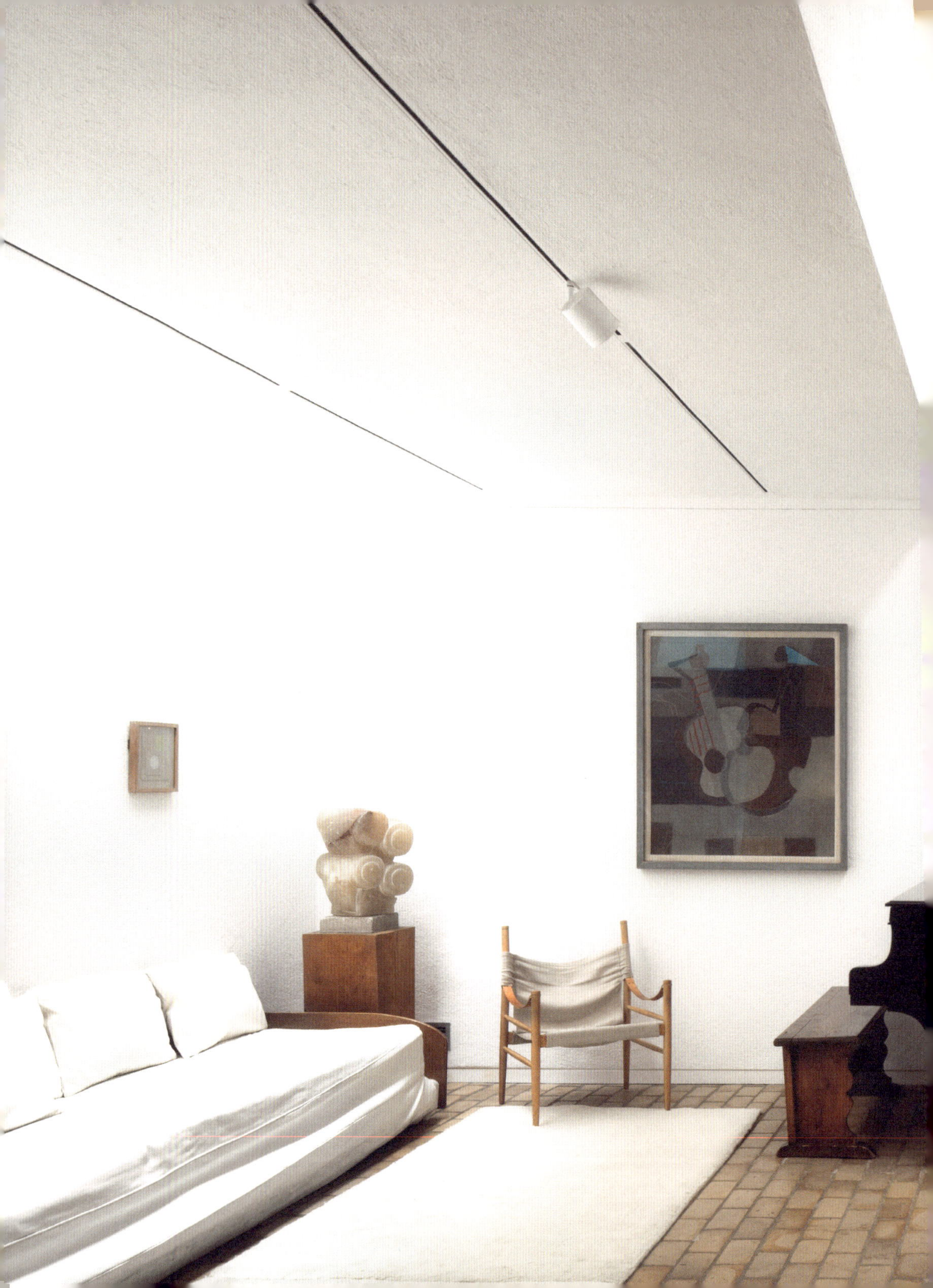

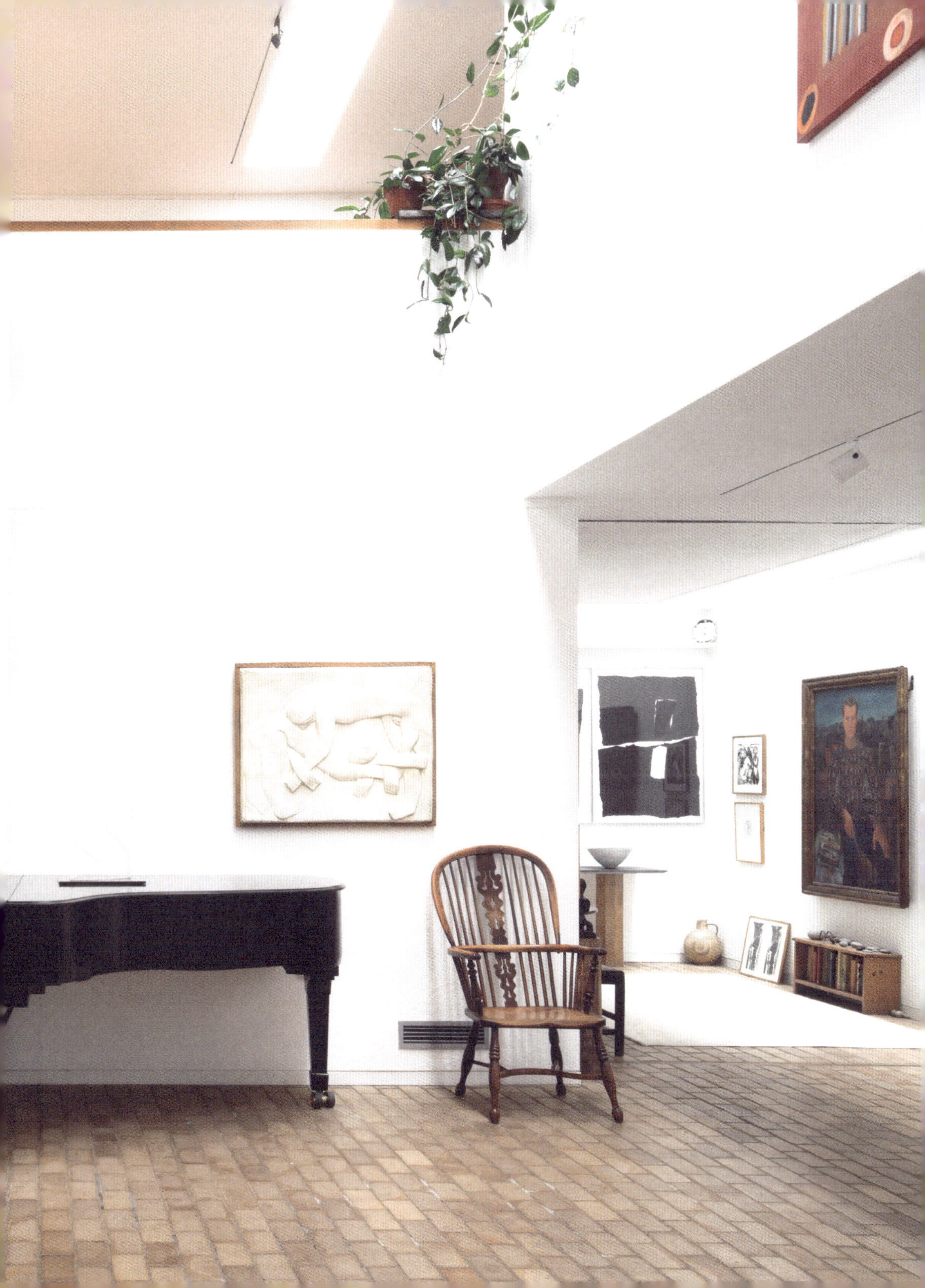

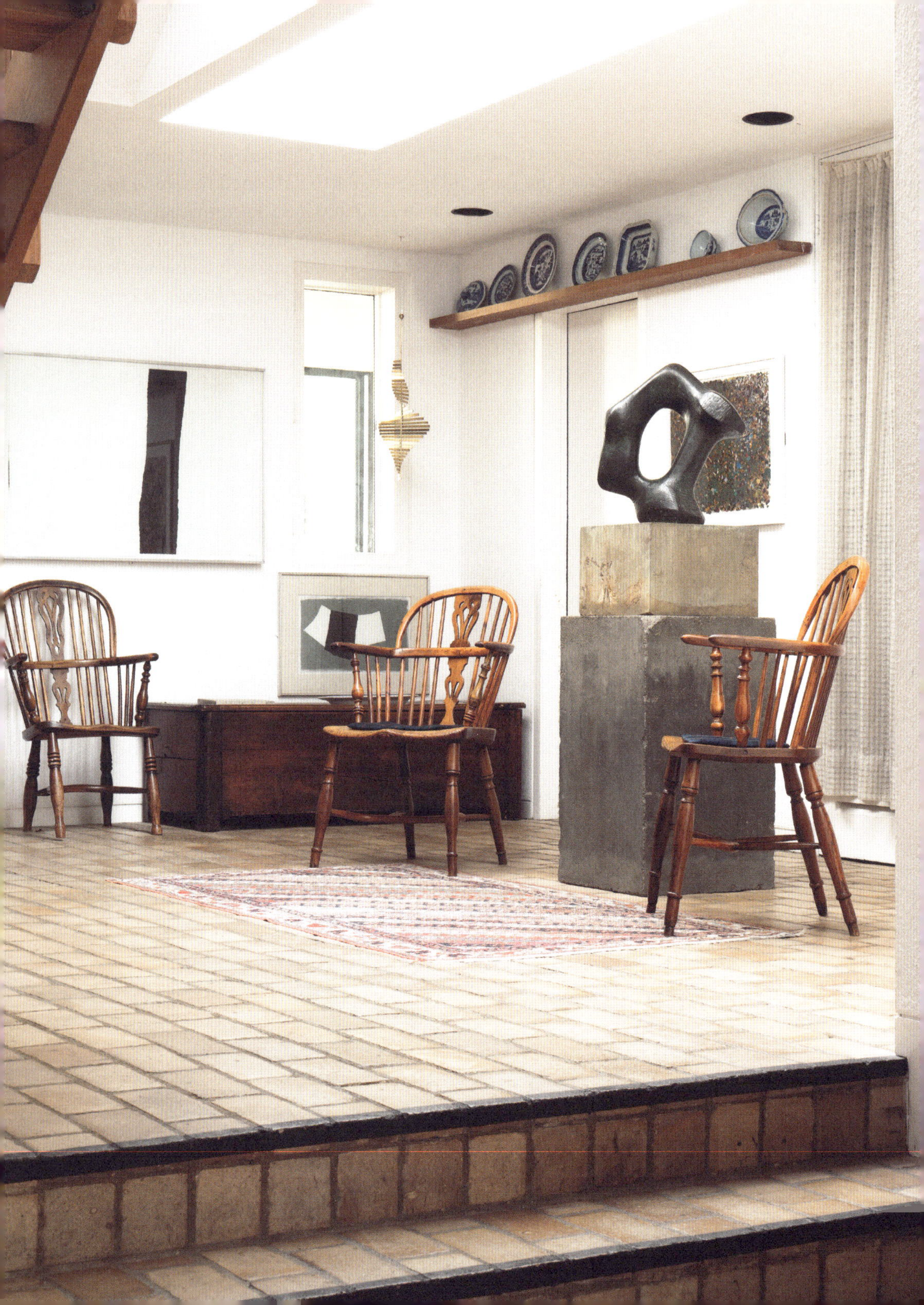

GROUND FLOOR 5

Under the open tread stairs is a piece of charred wood found by a friend of the Edes, John Catto. Catto darkened the wood to emphasise its human profile and named it St. Edmund before giving it to Jim Ede. This final space of the house includes a number of smaller works by Italo Valenti placed alongside a hanging work by Kenneth Martin and a bronze sculpture by Henry Moore. Having first met while the Edes were living in Hampstead in the 1920s, Jim Ede and Henry Moore reconnected at a party given by the publisher John Murray in 1956. Soon after, Jim Ede swapped a drawing by Henri Gaudier-Brzeska for Moore's small stone *Head* (located in Jim Ede's bedroom). In 1962, he purchased the bronze from an exhibition of Moore's work in Cambridge. At this time, Jim Ede was seeking Moore's advice on the posthumous casting of Gaudier-Brzeska's sculpture. This part of the house has been reconfigured since 1970 to accommodate changes to the building. Later additions include works by Avinash Chandra and Gillian Ayres. The high shelf displays a row of nineteenth-century blue and white porcelain that was in use by the Edes for several decades before being displayed in the extension. A late nineteenth-century rug originating from the South Caucasus region replaces similar earlier floor coverings.

1 Avinash Chandra
Untitled, 1964
Screenprint on card
KY00868.EH

2 Found object given to Jim Ede by John Catto
St. Edmund, 1975
Charred willow wood
KY01110.EH

3 David Peace
'And a river went out …', 1970
Engraved glass carboy
KY01001.EH

4 Flat-woven textile, Biskra, Algeria, undated
Wool
KY01103.EH

5 Italo Valenti
Nr. 145; Laguna; Lagune, 1968
Oil paint on canvas
KY01005.EH

6 Italo Valenti
Nr. 121; Olanda, 1968
Oil paint on canvas
KY01004.EH

7 Avinash Chandra
Black Feast, 1962
Ink and watercolour on paper
KY00793.EH

8 Henry Moore
Sculptural Object, 1960
Bronze on limestone base
KY00851.EH

9 Gillian Ayres
Untitled, 1972
Gouache and mixed media on paper
KY01387

10 Kenneth Martin
Screw Mobile, 1969
Brass
KY01018.EH

11 Italo Valenti
Nr. 380; Trinome, 1966
Paper collage on card
KY00920.EH

12 Eric Gill
My First Inscription (Jane Lister), c. 1903
Marble
KY01163.EH

13 Italo Valenti
Nr. 345; La Tua Ombra; Ton Ombre, 1966
Paper collage on paper
KY01007.EH

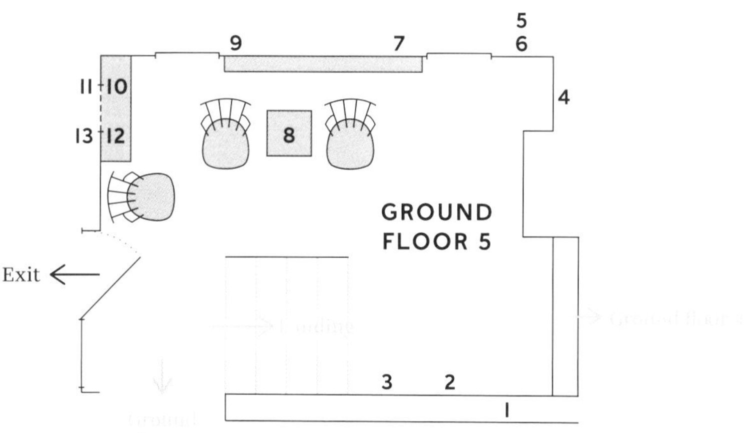

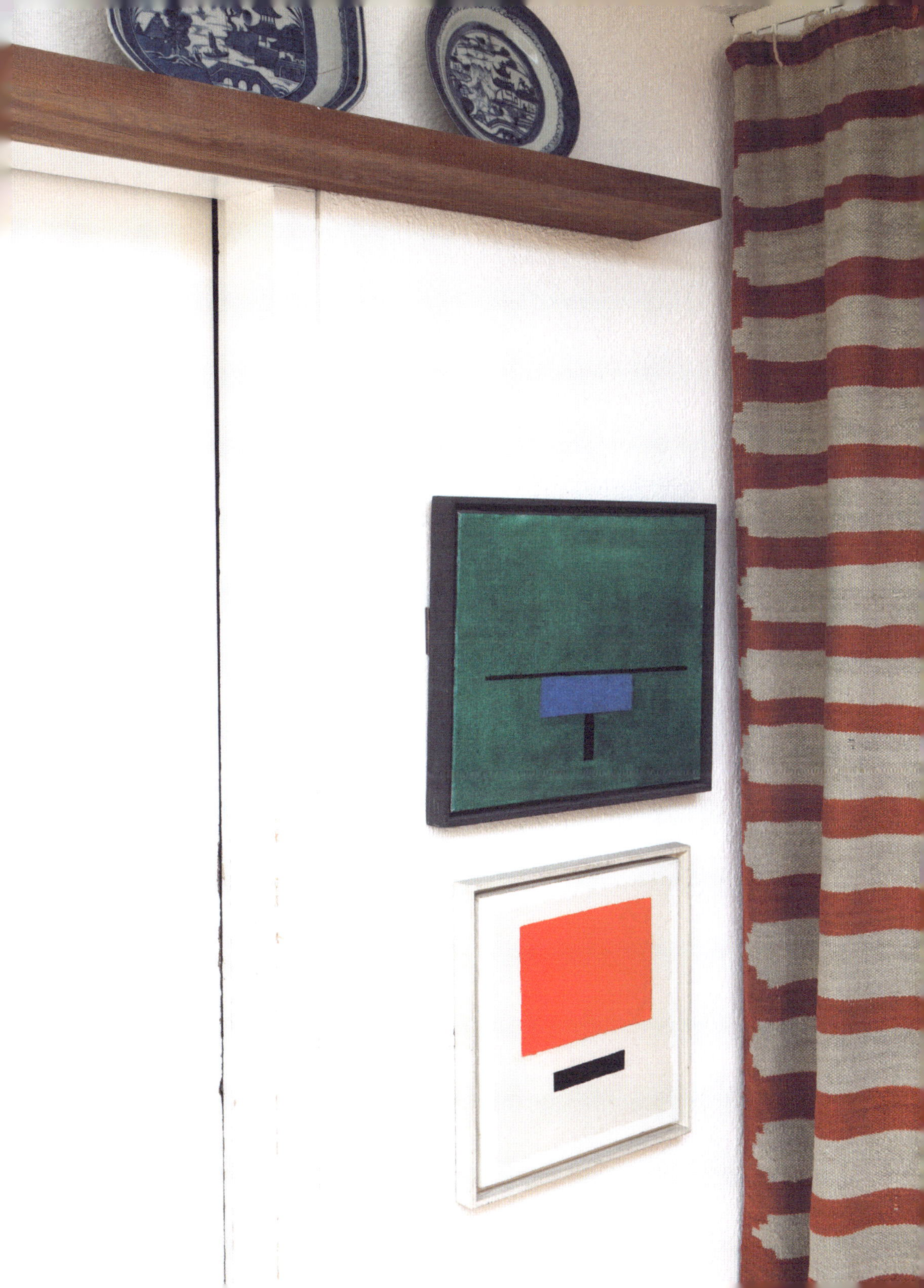

ARTIST BIOGRAPHIES

JOHN ACLAND (1940-2009) studied at Magdalene College, Cambridge, in the late 1950s and regularly visited Kettle's Yard.

JANE ADAMS (b.1949) is an artist and author who lives and works in London. She is a granddaughter of Jim and Helen Ede.

CAROLINE 'QUINCE' ADAMS (b. 1951) is an earthenware potter and sculptor. She is a granddaughter of Jim and Helen Ede.

FRANK AUERBACH (1931-2024) was born in Berlin and arrived in England aged eight as a refugee from Nazi Germany. In London he studied at St Martin's School of Art 1948-52 and the Royal College of Art 1952-55. In 1986 he represented Britain at the Venice Biennale. Auerbach's work at Kettle's Yard was purchased in the 1980s by the then curator, Jeremy Lewison.

GILLIAN AYRES (1930-2018) was known for her vibrantly coloured abstract paintings and prints which earned her a place on the 1989 Turner Prize shortlist. She held a number of teaching positions, at St Martins School of Art from 1965 to 1978, and as Head of Painting at Winchester School of Art until 1981. In 1987 she relocated to the North Devon-Cornwall border where she remained for the rest of her life. She was elected a Royal Academician in 1991.

JOHN BLACKBURN (1932-2022) trained at the Thanet and Maidenhead schools of art, specialising in textile design. After spending seven years in New Zealand, he settled near Canterbury in the UK. He exhibited at the John Moores Painting Prize exhibition at the Walker Art Gallery, Liverpool in 1961.

CONSTANTIN BRÂNÇUSI (1876-1957) was born in Hobiţa, Romania and trained at the Bucharest School of Fine Arts. In 1904 he moved to Paris, where he worked briefly in the workshop of Auguste Rodin. Brânçusi gradually evolved a pure, abstract manner that strove to depict the formal essence of objects without rejecting the natural world.

GEORGES BRAQUE (1882-1963) was born in Argenteuil, near Paris. By 1909 his close collaboration with Pablo Picasso had led to the evolution of a revolutionary approach to painting, subsequently called cubism. After the first world war, Braque returned to more naturalistic still life and figure compositions, aiming at a perfect balance and harmony between colour and design.

AVINASH CHANDRA (1931-91) was born in Shimla, India and studied at Delhi Polytechnic between 1947 and 1952, where he later taught. In 1956, he moved with his wife, Prem, to Golders Green in London. Chandra exhibited widely in the United States and the UK from the 1960s.

JOHN CLEGG (1935-2015) was born in Nottingham. After studying at the Leys School and Magdalene College in Cambridge, he worked as an archaeologist and lectured at Brisbane University, Australia alongside his work as a sculptor.

CECIL COLLINS (1908-1989) was born in Plymouth. He studied at the local art school (1924-27) and the Royal College of Art, London (1927-31). His work was concerned with religious and spiritual inquiry and was included in the International Surrealist Exhibition at the Burlington Galleries, London in 1936.

WILLIAM CONGDON (1912-98) was born in Rhode Island, USA, and studied at the Pennsylvania Academy of Fine Arts. After serving as an ambulance driver during the war, he settled in Italy and converted to Catholicism in 1959. He lived in Assisi in Italy in the 1960s and 1970s, painting a series of pictures of Venice and Subiaco. From 1979 he lived near Milan.

FRANCINE DEL PIERRE (1917-1971) was born in Paris, France. She exhibited her ceramics with Bernard Leach in Japan, and opened a studio in Vence in the South of France with Albert Diato. All of her work is coiled and in earthenware.

JAMES DIXON (1887-1970) was born on Tory Island, off the west coast of Ireland, where he spent his life working as a crofter and fisherman. He took up painting in the 1950s, having been encouraged to do so by the artist Derek Hill.

ZOË ELLISON (1916-1986) was born in Zimbabwe and studied at the Ewenny Pottery, Glamorgan and the Camberwell School of Arts and Crafts. She taught at the Cambridge School of Art and, with husband Jan, set up the Crosskeys Pottery in Cambridge.

MAX ERNST (1891-1976) was born in Brühl, near Cologne, Germany. After studying philosophy in Bonn, in 1913 he moved to Paris, where he was instrumental to the development of surrealism. He helped to organise the first surrealist exhibition in Paris in 1925. Ernst emigrated to the USA during the second world war.

NAUM GABO (1890-1977) was born in Bryansk, Russia. He lived in Berlin and Paris, where he and his brother, Antoine Pevsner, became leading exponents of constructivist art. In 1936 he moved to London, where he worked with Ben Nicholson, Barbara Hepworth, Leslie Martin and Sadie Speight on *Circle: International Survey of Constructive Art* (1937). During the war, he and his wife Miriam moved to St Ives and after to the USA.

HENRI GAUDIER-BRZESKA (1891-1915) was born in St Jean de Braye, near Orléans, in France. He met his partner Sophie Brzeska while working as a student at Sainte-Geneviève Library in Paris in 1910 and together they moved to London. There Gaudier-Brzeska associated with Ezra Pound, Wyndham Lewis and T.E. Hulme and exhibited with the vorticist group. He was killed in action during the first world war.

ERIC GILL (1882-1940) was born in Brighton. He was a sculptor, letter cutter, typeface designer and printmaker who ran the St. Dominic's Press from Ditchling, Sussex, where he lived for a time with David Jones. In 1989, Gill's biographer Fiona MacCarthy revealed the artist's history of abuse, with family members among his victims.

IAN HAMILTON FINLAY (1925-2006) was born in Nassau, Bahamas. He went to the Glasgow School of Art and joined the British army in 1942. At his home in Lanarkshire, Finlay created a garden filled with sculptural, landscape and poetic work on a range of themes.

BARBARA HEPWORTH (1903-1975) was born in Wakefield, Yorkshire and studied at the Leeds School of Art and the Royal College of Art in London. In 1924, she won a travel scholarship which enabled her to travel to Florence and in the 1930s she took part in various group exhibitions, including those of Abstraction-Création, the Seven and Five Society and Unit One. Hepworth lived in Cornwall from 1939 and showed her work internationally after the second world war.

LUBAINA HIMID (b. 1954) was born in Zanzibar, Tanzania and grew up in the UK. She studied theatre design at Wimbledon College of Art and cultural history at the Royal College of Art in London. Her work spans painting, drawing, installation, printmaking and curating, and engages with politics of race, gender and class. She won the Turner Prize in 2017 and was elected a Royal Academician in 2018.

ROGER HILTON (1911-1975) studied at the Slade School of Art, London and later at the Académie Ranson in Paris. After serving in the army during the second world war he enrolled at the Central School of Art in London. In 1965 he settled in St Ives and became known for his abstract paintings.

BRYAN ILLSLEY (1937-2024) lived in St Ives, Cornwall where he worked with the Leach Pottery. He subsequently lived and worked in Bermondsey, London as a sculptor, painter and jewellery maker.

DAVID JONES (1895-1974) was born in Brockley, London, and studied at the Camberwell School of Arts and Crafts before the first world war. He worked as an engraver and printer, while at the same time writing poetry and essays. His work reflects his interest in early Christianity, Arthurian myths and the ancient classical world.

EDMOND XAVIER KAPP (1890-1978) was a portrait painter, draughtsman and caricaturist. He went to Christ's College, Cambridge and in 1912 exhibited at the Fitzwilliam Museum. He was an official war artist 1940-41, and artist to UNESCO 1946-47.

GEORGE KENNETHSON (1910-1994) was born in Richmond, Surrey. After attending the Royal College of Art in London (1928-32), he became interested in sculpture made through direct carving. He exhibited regularly in London and Cambridge.

SIMON KENRICK (b.1943) studied architecture and history of art at Clare College, Cambridge. He is a specialist in Islamic art and architecture and teaches in California.

JIŘÍ KOLÁŘ (1914–2002) was born in Protivín, now in the Czech Republic. He began his career as a poet. In the 1950s his poems became more visual and in the 1960s Kolář worked with geometrical abstraction, visual poems and three-dimensional objects.

ISSAM KOURBAJ (b. 1963) was born in Syria and trained at the Institute of Fine Arts in Damascus, the Repin Institute of Fine Arts & Architecture in Leningrad (St Petersburg) and the Wimbledon School of Art. He has lived in Cambridge since 1990. From 2011, his work has related to the Syrian civil war, and reflects on the suffering of his fellow Syrians and the destruction of their cultural heritage.

L.S. LOWRY (1887–1976) was born in Manchester. He is best known for his paintings of northern industrial cities, expressing a sense of alienation. He occasionally painted views of the Lake District, as in the picture in Kettle's Yard.

WINSTON MCQUOID (1909–1984) was born in Glasgow. He attended art schools in Belfast, Northwich and London. His first solo show was held in Belfast in 1924, when he was only 14. He was a well-known portrait artist in the 1930s, with sitters including the writer, Osbert Sitwell.

OVIDIU MAITEC (1925–2006) was born in Arad, Romania. He studied at the Institutul de Arte Plastice, where he later also taught. Maitec recieved many public commissions in Romania and from the 1960s, his carved works became known in western Europe.

MARINO MARINI (1901–1980) was born in Pistoia, near Florence. A member of the Novecento group in the 1930s, he built up his international reputation with sculptures of animals and riders on horses. He was also a painter, lithographer and etcher.

KENNETH MARTIN (1905–84) was born in Sheffield. He studied at the Sheffield School of Art and the Royal College of Art, London. During the 1940s Martin's work began to emphasise elements of structure and design, and became purely abstract c. 1948. His work was included in the exhibition *This is Tomorrow* at the Whitechapel Gallery in London in 1956, and with his wife Mary and others, Martin was part of the revival of constructivism in the UK, after the second world war.

JOAN MIRÓ (1893–1983) was born in Barcelona, Spain. Between the first and second world wars he worked in Paris, where he associated with Pablo Picasso and the surrealists. Miró worked frequently with ceramics and printmaking as well as mural painting, and developed his own personal language of signs and symbols that were deeply rooted in his Catalan heritage.

HENRY MOORE (1898–1986) was born in Castleford, Yorkshire. He was a member of English modernist groups including the Seven and Five Society and Unit One, and his work was included in the International Surrealist Exhibition in London in 1936. Moore was an official war artist during the second world war, after which his work was exhibited and commissioned internationally.

WILLIAM STAITE MURRAY (1881-1962) was born in Deptford, London and trained at the Camberwell School of Arts and Crafts. He set up his own pottery in 1919, and his work was often shown alongside modern forms of painting and sculpture, including at the Seven and Five Society annual exhibitions.

BEN NICHOLSON (1894-1982) travelled between Cumberland, London, Paris and Switzerland throughout the 1920s, often with his wife, Winifred Nicholson. Between 1931 and 1939 he lived in London and met artists and critics such as Henry Moore, John Piper, Leslie Martin, Herbert Read and Barbara Hepworth (who became his second wife in 1938). Nicholson developed a highly abstract style in the 1930s. He returned to St Ives during the second world war and exhibited internationally in the 1950s and 60s.

KATE NICHOLSON (1929-2019) was the daughter of Ben and Winifred Nicholson. She studied at the Bath Academy of Art and in 1957 moved to St Ives. Her work was exhibited at the Waddington Gallery and the Marjorie Parr Gallery in London and at the LYC Museum and Art Gallery in Cumbria.

SIMON NICHOLSON (1934-1990) was the son of Ben Nicholson and Barbara Hepworth. He studied sculpture at the Royal College of Art in London, and archaeology and anthropology at Trinity College, Cambridge. He lived and worked in St Ives, Cornwall and in the USA, teaching at the University of Berkeley, California.

WINIFRED NICHOLSON (1893-1981) was born in Oxford. She studied in London and exhibited with her husband, Ben Nicholson, in the 1920s, including as a member of the Seven and Five Society. In 1937 she contributed an essay on painting to the landmark publication *Circle: International Survey of Constructive Art*. After the war she settled permanently at the house in Cumberland she had bought in 1924.

CORNELIA PARKER (b. 1956) was born in Cheshire. She studied at Wolverhampton Polytechnic and the University of Reading. Her sculpture and installation work explores destruction, resurrection and reconfiguration. She was shortlisted for the Turner Prize in 1997 and in 2010 was elected a Royal Academician.

VICKEN PARSONS (b. 1957) studied at the Slade School of Fine Art, London. She makes small, intimate paintings on wood panel using thin layers of oil paint. Her subjects are usually of landscapes or architectural spaces, some remembered and others imagined.

DAVID PEACE (1915-2003) was born in Sheffield, and lived and worked near Cambridge. His glass engravings are held in many collections, including the Victoria and Albert Museum. He was the first chairman of the Guild of Glass Engravers.

BRYAN PEARCE (1929-2007) was born in St Ives and studied at the St Ives School of Painting 1953-57. He exhibited with the Penwith Society and met Jim Ede through Barbara Hepworth.

MICHAEL PINE (1928–2013) was born in Wolverhampton and studied architecture in Birmingham. His papier-mâché 'bubble' sculptures were included in the 1956 exhibition *This is Tomorrow* at the Whitechapel Gallery in London. He later lived in St Ives, Cornwall and in Ottawa, Canada.

KATHERINE PLEYDELL-BOUVERIE (1895–1985) trained at the Central School of Arts and Crafts, London. In 1924 she became one of Bernard Leach's first students in St Ives. After a year there, she started her own workshop, the Cole Pottery, in Berkshire. She became well known for her work with ash glazes.

RICHARD POUSETTE-DART (1916–1992) was born in Minnesota. During the 1940s he became associated with abstract expressionism. He practiced sculpture, painting and photography, and taught at various institutions, including Columbia University.

LUCIE RIE (1902–1995) was born in Vienna, Austria. After training at the Kunstgewerbeschulen, she moved to England in 1938 and established a studio at Albion Mews in London where she worked for the rest of her life. Among her studio assistants was Hans Coper, who she taught with at Camberwell School of Arts and Crafts.

ABANI ROY (1904–1975) was born in Bengal, India prior to partition, and trained as an artist in Kolkata. He came to know the Edes in Hampstead, London. In 1931 Roy created an engraving documenting the historic Round Table Conference on India in London at St. James's Palace. He exhibited at the Royal Academy in the 1930s.

WILLIAM SCOTT (1913–1989) trained at the Belfast School of Art and, in 1932, moved to London to study at the Royal Academy Schools. After war service he moved to Somerset, and developed an abstract style of printing. From the mid-1950s he received many large-scale commissions.

MARIO SIRONI (1885–1961) was born in Sassari, Sardinia in Italy. He studied in Rome and came into contact with the futurists. He was later influenced by the 'Pittura Metafisica' movement. He was a founder member of the Novecento group in 1922, and painted numerous frescoes, including those for the University of Rome.

SOPHIE TAEUBER-ARP (1889–1943) was born in Switzerland, and began her career studying textile design and modern dance. She moved to Zürich in 1915, met Dada artist Hans Arp and designed sets, costumes and puppets for Dada performances at the Cabaret Voltaire. Taeuber-Arp lived in Paris from the late 1920s, continuing her architectural and design work. In the 1930s, she made abstract paintings and wood reliefs, and was associated with the Cercle et Carré and Abstraction Création groups.

KENJI UMEDA (1948-2019) was born in Japan. While in Cambridge in the early 1970s he helped Jim Ede with housework at Kettle's Yard. He became interested in sculpture at this time, and gained a scholarship to study in Carrara, Italy. From there he moved to Arizona, USA, where he continued his sculpture practice.

ITALO VALENTI (1912-1995) was born in Milan, Italy. He lived and worked in Italy and Switzerland, and his work was also exhibited in the United States, Britain and Germany. He was introduced to Jim Ede by Ben Nicholson.

GREGORIO VARDANEGA (1923-2007) was born in Italy and grew up in Argentina. He studied in Buenos Aires and was a member of the Asociación Arte Concreto-Invención (AACI). He exhibited in Europe in the 1950s, and settled in Paris with his wife, artist Martha Boto.

ELISABETH VELLACOTT (1905-2002) attended the Royal College of Art in London between 1925 and 1929. At the beginning of her career, she worked as a textile and theatrical designer. She was a founder member of the Cambridge Society of Painters and Sculptors in 1954. She exhibited regularly in London and at Kettle's Yard in 1981 and 1995.

ALFRED WALLIS (1855-1942) was born in Devon. He was a fisherman and later ran a shop in St Ives, Cornwall trading in second-hand goods and scrap. After the death of his wife in 1922 he turned to painting. He was admired by Ben Nicholson and Christopher Wood, who met him when visiting St Ives in 1928. Wallis's paintings were included in the Seven and Five Society exhibition of 1929.

LAURENCE WHISTLER (1912-2000) was a glass engraver and poet. He was the first President of the British Guild of Glass Engravers as well as the first recipient of the King's Gold Medal for Poetry.

CHRISTOPHER WOOD (1901-1930) was born near Liverpool and first visited Paris in 1921. In France, he met artists such as Pablo Picasso and Jean Cocteau and worked on designs for a Ballets Russes production of *Romeo and Juliet*. In England, he became close friends with Ben and Winifred Nicholson. He visited Brittany in 1929 and 1930, where he made his final paintings.

LI YUAN-CHIA (1929-1994) was born in Guangxi, China. He studied art at the Taipei Normal College for Teacher Training, and became a member of the Ton Fan Group in Taiwan in 1956. In the 1960s, he moved to Italy and then Britain, where he showed with the Lisson Gallery in London. In 1972 he converted a rundown farmhouse at Banks on Hadrian's Wall, Cumbria into his own gallery, the LYC Museum.

FURTHER READING

- Inga Fraser, *Kettle's Yard Art & Artists* (Cambridge: Kettle's Yard, 2026)
- Laura Freeman, *Ways of Life: Jim Ede and the Kettle's Yard Artists* (London: Jonathan Cape, 2023)
- H.S. Ede, *A way of life: Kettle's Yard* (Cambridge: University of Cambridge Press, 1984)

PHOTOGRAPHING KETTLE'S YARD

What is unique about Kettle's Yard is that it encourages you to look. It does not instruct you how to see. There are no labels to guide you, no glass cases separating you from the objects. Instead, you are free to encounter the house at your own pace - to move through it slowly and, in doing so, to become part of its composition.

You are invited to sit, to pause, to stay awhile, to breathe in the place. To reflect while surrounded by art, found objects, worn surfaces and chipped crockery. As you settle, you begin to sense the vibration between these things, and your own presence folds into the house and its accumulated stories.

Over several months, I returned to Kettle's Yard again and again to make the photographs for this guidebook, living with the house through changing light and seasons. I came to celebrate the space between things - the way objects and rooms hold one another in balance. Whether working close to the floor, from high on a step ladder, or folded quietly beneath the piano, each position offered me a different way of seeing and of being - what Jim Ede referred to as the sacrament of the present.

I took, from my time here, that there is no right or wrong way to experience the house. It does not ask you to arrive with knowledge or be well read. It simply asks that you come in, open your eyes and give yourself time to enjoy the moment.

I hope, through these photographs, you discover your own way of looking at the house and experiencing Kettle's Yard.

— Gilbert McCarragher, Photographer, 2026

ACKNOWLEDGEMENTS

The first catalogue of the works on display at Kettle's Yard was published as a supplement to *Granta*, vol. 73, no. 3, February 1968. It was edited by Keith Moffat with photography by John Haselgrove, both students at King's College, Cambridge at the time. A bibliography by Duncan Robinson, then a student at Clare College, Cambridge was also included. Jim Ede wrote an introduction which has been retained in all subsequent catalogues and guidebooks to date.

A second catalogue was published in 1970, to cover the rearrangement of the collection following the opening of the Martin-Owers extension. This was edited by Duncan Robinson and his wife, Lisa (née Elizabeth Anne Sutton). A third catalogue, *Kettle's Yard: An Illustrated Guide* was published in 1980, edited by Jeremy Lewison, who was the curator of Kettle's Yard 1977–1983. Lewison's text was the basis for the updated catalogue, *Kettle's Yard House Guide*, which was first published in 2002 and included a new history of Kettle's Yard by Sebastiano Barassi, curator of collections 2001–2012. This was updated and redesigned in 2018 by Jennifer Powell, then head of collection and programme.

The present *Kettle's Yard House Guidebook* preserves Jim Ede's original introduction and revises and extends Barassi's history of the house and collection. It is accompanied by a sister publication, *Kettle's Yard Art & Artists* which collects Ede's writings and letters to and from the artists in the collection. In the making of these new books, we acknowledge the research and writing of previous Kettle's Yard curators and assistants, without whom the current publications could not have been made. The support from artists' estates has also been integral to the project, and is hugely appreciated. Special thanks to Gilbert McCarragher for a wonderful new set of photographs of the house and collection; to designer Mark El-khatib for realising the new guidebook with style and clarity; to Sam McGuire, for her astute copy and line edits; and to Laura Pryke, retail and publications manager, for supporting and guiding the process with patience and good humour throughout. Thank you also to Shikha Dwivedi, administration and reporting assistant who has worked tirelessly to research and obtain rights and permissions; to Gabrielle Brasier, assistant curator; Beth Darbyshire, archivist; Tom Noblett, programme technician; and to volunteer publication assistants Florence Austin, Heather Boswell, Yasemin Gyford, Katie

Maynard and Sid White-Jones. I am also grateful to all Kettle's Yard staff who have passed on their knowledge of the plants, flowers and furniture at Kettle's Yard, including Shirley-Anne McAndrew, Sabrina Rippon and Andrew Smith; and to facilities and security manager Steve Penney and receptionist Christine Cowling-Jones who have facilitated the new photography of the house. Finally, the vast majority of artworks and objects listed in this book were - of course - acquired by Jim and Helen Ede; but here I would also like to thank all those individuals and organisations who have given or funded the purchase of items for the collection acquired subsequently, not least the Friends and Patrons of Kettle's Yard.

— Inga Fraser, Senior Curator, 2026

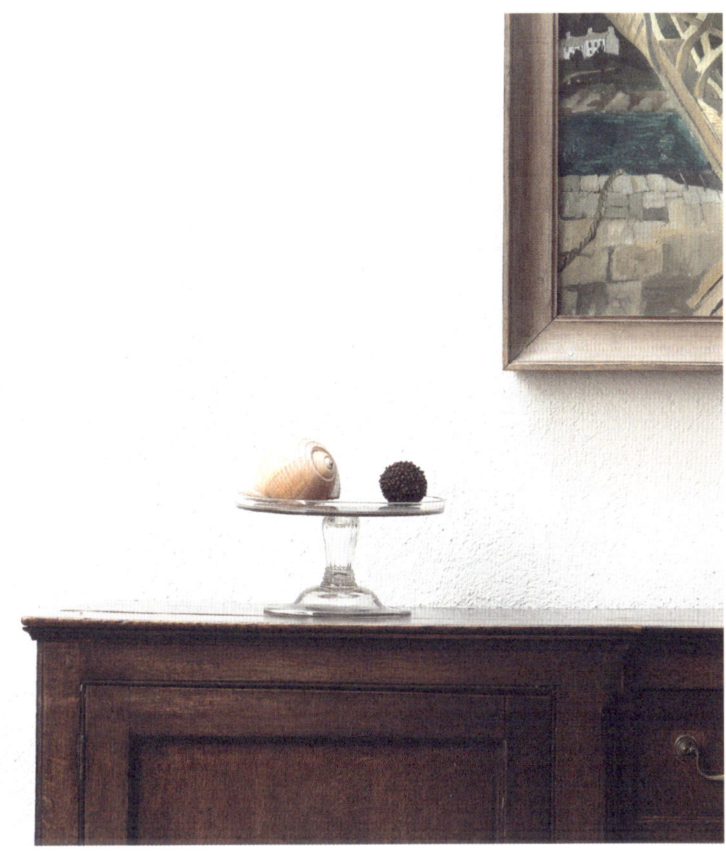

KETTLE'S YARD HOUSE GUIDEBOOK
Published by Kettle's Yard
University of Cambridge, 2026

Kettle's Yard
Castle Street, Cambridge CB3 0AQ
kettlesyard.cam.ac.uk
Director: Andrew Nairne OBE
Assistant Director: Susie Biller
Chair: Sonita Alleyne OBE

ISBN 978-1-90456-161-3

Distributed in the UK, Europe and the rest of the world by ACC Art Books, Riverside House, Dock Lane, Melton, Woodbridge, Suffolk IP12 1PE
accartbooks.com

EU Authorised Representative: Easy Access System Europe - Mustamäe tee 50, 10621 Tallinn, Estonia
gpsr.requests@easproject.com

Every effort has been made to ensure images are correctly attributed however if any omission or error has been made please notify the publisher for correction in future editions.

KETTLE'S YARD

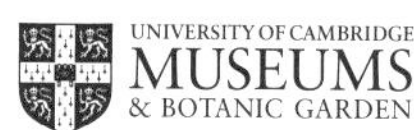

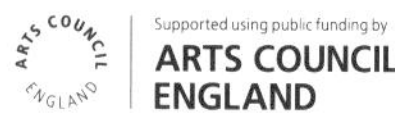

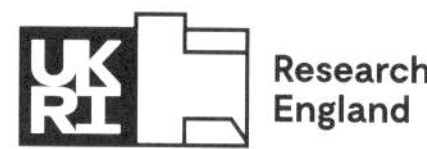

Written and edited by Inga Fraser
Copyedited by Sam McGuire
Publication managed by Laura Pryke
Photography by Gilbert McCarragher
Design by Mark El-khatib studio
Printed by Taylor Brothers, Bristol

CREDITS

Cover: Gregorio Vardanega, *Disc*, c. 1960. Photo: Gilbert McCarragher
p. 8 Photo: Derry Moore © Derry Moore.
p. 12 Photographer unknown. Photo courtesy Kettle's Yard, University of Cambridge.
p. 14 Photographer unknown. Photo courtesy of Mary Adams.
p. 17-21 Photographers unknown, except p. 17 (below) Studio Casa Ros. All photos courtesy Kettle's Yard, University of Cambridge
p. 22-23 © Kettle's Yard, University of Cambridge.
p. 24 Photo: Chris Hurst. Courtesy Kettle's Yard, University of Cambridge.
pp. 4, 6, 27, 28, 30, 32, 36-37, 38, 42, 46, 48-49, 52, 55, 57, 58-59, 60, 64-65, 66, 69, 72-73, 74, 78-79, 80, 84-85, 86, 90-91, 94-95, 98-99, 100, 104-105, 106, 109, 119 © Gilbert McCarragher.
pp. 30, 57 Courtesy of Kettle's Yard, University of Cambridge.
p. 32, 60 © The William G. Congdon Foundation, Milano, Italy congdonfoundation.com.
p. 66 © Jacqueline Benard.
pp. 72-74, 90-91 © Trustees of Winifred Nicholson.
p. 109 © Estate of Italo Valenti.
Inside cover quote by Lubaina Himid from *A Way of Living: Kettle's Yard* (dir. Chris Vale)

SUPPORT US

Donate or become a member today and help us care for the house and collection, organise exhibitions and engage children, young people and community groups in our work.

Find out more about how you can help:
kettlesyard.cam.ac.uk/join-support/
development@kettlesyard.cam.ac.uk
01223 748100